Protecting the Social Service Client

Legal and Structural Controls
on Official Discretion

JOEL F. HANDLER

Institute for Research on Poverty
University of Wisconsin—Madison
Madison, Wisconsin

ACADEMIC PRESS   New York   San Francisco   London
A Subsidiary of Harcourt Brace Jovanovich, Publishers

This book is one of a series sponsored by the Institute for Research on Poverty of the University of Wisconsin pursuant to the provisions of the Economic Opportunity Act of 1964.

ACADEMIC PRESS, INC.
111 Fifth Avenue, New York, New York 10003

United Kingdom Edition published by
ACADEMIC PRESS, INC. (LONDON) LTD.
24/28 Oval Road, London NW1

Library of Congress Cataloging in Publication Data

Handler, Joel F.
Protecting the social service client.

(Poverty policy analysis series ; 5)
Bibliography: p.
1. Public welfare--Law and legislation--United States.
2. Social service--United States. I. Title. II. Se-
ries.
KF3721.H36 1979   344'.73'031   78-22528
ISBN 0-12-322842-5 (cloth)
ISBN 0-12-322848-7 (paper)

PRINTED IN THE UNITED STATES OF AMERICA

79 80 81 82   9 8 7 6 5 4 3 2 1

For Betsy

Contents

6
Structural Alternatives

The Institute for Research on Poverty is a national center for research established at the University of Wisconsin in 1966 by a grant from the Office of Economic Opportunity. Its primary objective is to foster basic, multidisciplinary research into the nature and causes of poverty and means to combat it.

In addition to increasing the basic knowledge from which policies aimed at the elimination of poverty can be shaped, the Institute strives to carry analysis beyond the formulation and testing of fundamental generalizations to the development and assessment of relevant policy alternatives.

The Institute endeavors to bring together scholars of the highest caliber whose primary research efforts are focused on the problem of poverty, the distribution of income, and the analysis and evaluation of social policy, offering staff members wide opportunity for interchange of ideas, maximum freedom for research into basic questions about poverty and social policy, and dissemination of their findings.

Foreword

During the 1960s, the legal profession became quite concerned about the legal rights of government agency clients. This concern was a part of the War on Poverty since many of the clients were (are) poor. Reform activity reached its zenith in 1970 when the U.S. Supreme Court in *Goldberg* vs. *Kelly* held that the Due Process Clause of the Constitution applied to welfare hearings. Subsequently, there was an eightfold increase in AFDC hearings. The Social Security Administration now has a fair hearing caseload of 150,000 per year. This dramatic increase in administrative hearings led to calls for reform. In decisions subsequent to *Goldberg* the Supreme Court reduced the procedural formality necessary in social welfare hearings. Congress has called for a reexamination of the Social Security Administration hearings. The legal rights of clients are now obviously in a state of flux.

In this context, Joel Handler's *Protecting the Social Service Client: Legal and Structural Controls on Official Discretion* is quite timely. Handler examines the treatment of clients of public and private social service agencies and concludes that the existence and abuse of administrative discretion necessitate consumer protection. Handler's particular concern is the legal rights of these social service clients, and he questions how effectively these rights are being enforced. Concentrating on the abuses of administrative discretion, he describes the history of due process protection (i.e., by means of appeals and court hearings) and offers a number of legal and structural remedies.

Though the main focus of the book is on social service agencies and their clients—principally the poor, as Handler notes in his Preface—the issues addressed have much wider applicability. Every one of us is likely to find ourselves at one time or another confronting a representative of a government agency who has the discretionary authority to grant or withhold benefits.

This volume is part of an ongoing research effort at the Institute for Research on Poverty on legal and administrative systems and the poor. Handler himself has contributed a large portion of this research. Indeed, *Protecting the Social Service Client* is the culmination of over a decade of his research. By drawing on new data, focusing on the sources of the discretionary behavior, and proposing changes in present systems, this book extends the work published in two previous studies, *The Deserving Poor* (with Ellen Jane Hollingsworth) and *The Coercive Social Worker.*

Irwin Garfinkel
Director, Institute for Research on Poverty

Preface: The Need for a New Look

This book is about consumer protection. The consumers are the clients of public and private social service agencies that deliver publicly financed goods and services. I am concerned with the legal rights of these consumers, how well or how poorly these rights are respected and enforced, and what can be done to strengthen them. Such issues are of obvious concern to those who have long fought for the rights of the poor, but they also have broader applicability. Social service agencies serve the nonpoor as well as the poor; more importantly, the problems clients face in dealing with social services are representative of the wider class of issues that all citizens face when they confront discretionary administration throughout government. Although the specific focus of this book is on the delivery of social services, the analysis and proposed remedies are applicable to any program characterized by a high degree of administrative discretion and a dependent clientele. My audience, then, includes not only advocates for social service and welfare clients, but also those who are fighting for the rights of people who deal with the health and mental health systems, the school system, special education, employment programs, and other social welfare agencies.

Because the issues affect the consumers of many government services, this book should also be of interest to those on the other side—social workers and other professionals who work in these agencies, bureaucrats and supervisory personnel, and policymakers. Client protection is part of a broad advocacy movement on behalf of the underdog that is by now more than 20 years old; its roots go back to the civil rights struggles of the 1950s and 1960s, the War on Poverty, Ralph Nader and consumerism, and its latest manifestation, public interest law. Consumer and client protection is a multifaceted field that draws upon diverse sources of support. Some of its principal allies, such as Legal Services, have survived periods of political attack and financial retrenchment, although other supporters, such as the National Welfare Rights Organization, have fallen on hard times. Although it is not my intention to exaggerate the strength of this broad movement, it should not be dismissed as a passing phenomenon of the American political scene. Concern for the legal rights of consumers has struck a responsive chord in the political life of the country and has been seized upon by ambitious politicians. In the past decade, for example, dozens of consumer protection and civil liberties measures have been enacted into law, and client influences have also been felt in the administration of social services and other social welfare programs. Therefore, if only out of self-interest, those who devise and administer programs for the poor and dependent ought to be interested in how their actions are viewed by consumer advocates.

It is hoped, of course, that social work professionals, administrators, and policymakers will view the issues of client protection in a more affirmative light. The concern for the legal rights of citizens reflects normative judgments about basic social justice and the belief that all people should be viewed as human beings worthy of respect and fair and equal treatment by their government. It is not always apparent how these rights are defined and, more importantly, how they can become subverted in the course of administration. It is also not readily apparent how legal protections can be rendered ineffective by the social context in which they operate. One need not be a partisan to be concerned with basic rights and the just and humane treatment of those who deal with their government.

Recent developments in the law and in social welfare programs call for a new look at existing methods of protecting clients dependent on social welfare programs and agencies. As I discuss more fully in later chapters, 1970 was the watershed year for advocates of the poor. In *Goldberg v. Kelly,* the Supreme Court held that the Due Process Clause of the Constitution applied to welfare hearings. The *Goldberg* principles were applied to a variety of other appeal situations in schools, prisons, parole proceedings, and social welfare programs. It looked as if those who had been long struggling for the legal protection of the poor and minorities would prevail.

Soon after the *Goldberg* ruling there was a sharp rise in administrative hearings; cries of anguish arose that the federal judiciary had gone too far, that clients were taking advantage of, if not abusing, legal protections, and that administration was breaking down. The attack on due process rights extends beyond welfare and questions the basic due process model in other contexts such as administrative economic regulation, the criminal justice system, civil litigation, and family matters. Part of the call for reform comes from those who think that we have become excessive in protecting individual rights at the expense of society—that we have sacrificed efficiency through an excessive concern for fairness. They call for a cutback on procedural protections and access to courts and administrative hearings. Others take the opposite view, namely, that the increase in hearings and court cases reflects an underlying need for the airing of legitimate grievances and that existing procedures have to be strengthened to improve legal protections.

Whatever position one takes, it is clear that we are in a period of crisis and change. All systems of conflict resolution are struggling under enormous loads. Aid to Families with Dependent Children (AFDC) has had an eightfold increase in hearings since *Goldberg* v. *Kelly,* and other agencies have experienced similar increases. The Social Security Administration is staggering under a load of more than 150,000 hearings per year.

Not unexpectedly, these pressures on the system have caused concern and demands for change. The Supreme Court itself has led the way; it has retreated from the *Goldberg* decision and reduced the procedural formality necessary in social welfare hearings. There are calls for reconsideration from other quarters as well. The states have demanded that the Department of Health, Education, and Welfare relax its hearing rules for social services, and Congress has called for a reexamination of Social Security Administration hearings, as well as hearings in other regulatory agencies.

We are entering, then, a period where traditional views about legal protections for dependent clients are being reexamined and are likely to undergo considerable change. Those who are concerned for the plight of the downtrodden in American society—the poor and minorities—can no longer count on the Supreme Court and the federal judiciary to uphold the values of the Due Process Clause in order to provide, at least in theory, maximum protection for the client. But it must also be recognized that the due process model, whatever lofty ideals it may contain, is simply not adequate to protect clients. A search must begin for more efficient procedures; the present approach is not satisfactory either to the clients or to the administrators.

At the same time that legal procedures are being reconsidered, there also have been significant changes in our welfare programs. The adult categories in the Social Security system have been merged, and there has been an enormous growth in the Social Security disability program. There is a new social services program, and President Carter has recently announced a proposed new income-maintenance and jobs program. Changes have been suggested in the Food Stamp program, Medicaid, Medicare, and work programs, and national health insurance has been proposed. These programs involve varying degrees of discretionary authority over clients and varying needs for client protection. As programs are modified or introduced, there are new opportunities to devise better procedures to protect client rights. For example, HEW, under pressure from the states, is reconsidering the hearing regulations of Title XX, the new social services program, in light of recent Supreme Court changes and demands from the states for more flexible procedures. There has been extensive study of the Social Security Administration disability hearings. We can expect similar demands to be made for hearing procedures in other programs as well.

Because of the dissatisfaction with existing methods of client protection and the impending changes in social welfare programs, this is an opportune time to review the experience of client protections in social welfare systems and suggest new approaches in light of that experience. This book uses as its focal point Title XX, the new social service program, but as the subsequent discussion will show, the issues of discretion and legal protection illustrated in the context of social services apply more generally. Indeed, many of the research findings and illustrations are drawn from other programs.

Although the book's main concern is protecting clients in their dealings with social services agencies, it attempts to place the discussion in perspective. Client protections, if they are to be effective, have to take into account the demands of government. It is futile to call for client protections that society cannot afford or that no government program could incorporate. Even more importantly, effective client remedies depend on other reforms in the system. The acceptability as well as the implementation of complementary reforms depends on agents other than clients and their advocates. Thus, although traditional client protections can be strengthened, alternative strategies and structural reforms have to be considered as well.

The book is divided into two parts. Part I, "The Issues: Discretion and Due Process Protection," sets forth the issues and reviews the experiences of client protections under the due process model. The problem is defined in Chapter 1. From the perspective of the law, the problem facing social service clients can be summed up in the word "discretion." What are the reasons for agency discretion? What produces discretion, and why is the law concerned with discretion? Chapter 2 is concerned with legal theory—how constitutional and statutory law defines the legal interests of social service clients and what system of protection the law provides. As this chapter shows, the law is in flux and seeks an accommodation between the interests of the client and the demands of administration. Chapter 3 examines the protection of client rights in practice. The legal system of rights does not operate in a vacuum; it is constrained and shaped by its social context—the bureaucracy, the clients, the structure of the rules, and the available resources. The social context seriously weakens whatever protection the law affords social services clients.

The lessons to be drawn from the theory and practice of due process legal protection are then applied in Part II "Legal and Structural Remedies," which discusses several different legal and structural approaches to client protections. Many of the remedies in Chapters 4, 5, and 6 are drawn from other fields and are in the experimental stage; some have been in operation for varying periods of time; others are only proposals. Although existing experience and issues are discussed, whether the suggestions in Part II will prove fruitful will, inevitably, depend on further research and experimentation.

In Chapter 4, the focus is still on the legal protection of clients from the client perspective, and alternative methods of strengthening client resources are discussed. Chapters 5 and 6 shift the focus from the point of view of the client to that of the policymaker. The first issue is the relationship of management and quality control to client protection. Although supervisory control systems are not usually viewed from this perspective, they bear on client rights in at least two important respects. To the extent that control systems can reduce error, the task of protecting clients should be lessened; but to the extent that ill-conceived or ill-executed control systems distort administration, they can increase problems of client protection. The second important issue, which is very serious and promises to become even more so in the future, is the conflict between information gathering for control and budgetary purposes and the privacy interests of clients. This, again, is a concern that obviously extends beyond social service clients.

Chapter 6 deals with structural reform. It has two major themes. One is the relationship between problems of controlling administrative discretion on the one hand, and program goals and the language of rules on the other. The second theme is the relation between control of discretion and the structure of the delivery system; the choice is between integrating the delivery system, which will increase discretion, and introducing more competitive elements to reduce discretion. Again, as in other chapters, trade-offs are discussed and proposals are offered.

The book is concerned with legal and structural remedies; it does not discuss another obvious potential remedy for clients—the organization of client groups to disseminate information and to demand and enforce their legal rights. There are several reasons for this omission. There is, by now, a considerable literature on the organization of the poor and minorities, and the interested reader can quite easily learn the history, problems, and potential of this approach. A second reason is that I think that those who have argued for the organization of clients have focused too heavily on a strict or legalistic due process model for the protection of clients. More attention ought to be placed on trying to control discretion at its source rather than relying so heavily on client advocacy to combat the effects of discretion. In view of the great difficulties in mobilizing the poor, another focus is needed. A third reason is that the two approaches are not inconsistent. Whatever legal and structural reforms are adopted, discretion will still remain in varying amounts and clients will still need advocacy protections. Clients will invariably be better off if they have the support of a strong organization. The omission of client organization, then, should not be interpreted as a rejection of that alternative; rather, the purpose of this book is to promote the need for other, less obvious methods of protecting clients.

Controlling administrative discretion is a problem throughout government, but it is an especially acute problem for lower-income people. The poorer the people and the more reliant upon agencies, the more severe are the problems of administrative justice. The difficulties that the poor encounter with social service agencies are manifest in schools, hospitals, mental institutions, prisons, and training programs, although the intensity of the problem may vary from agency to agency. Moreover, the direction of social welfare policy does not bode well for the lessening of official discretionary controls. There seems to be no slackening in the numbers of people destined to spend their last years in nursing homes. Increasing health care will also carry with it the burdens of increased discretionary control, as will the substitution of in-kind programs and services for cash assistance, and a renewed emphasis on work. The plight of the poor in a great many administrative systems is serious and pervasive.

I attempt to address the issue of administrative or procedural justice without regard to substantive justice or questions of income redistribution. The dependency of clients upon social services and similar agencies stems in large measure from their poverty. The way they are treated by government reflects paternalistic, hostile, or indifferent administrative and social attitudes toward the poor. We might then ask to what extent people can be treated equally before the law when they suffer such inequality in life. Perhaps there is no satisfactory answer to this question. The poor suffer day by day in the systems they deal with and need help with these daily problems, just as they need medical attention even though, in the long run, better health would be accomplished through improved diet, housing, sanitation, and education. At the present time, the prospects for the poor do not seem hopeful. In the meantime, we can become more sensitive to the problems of administrative justice that they face in everyday life, resist exacerbations of those problems, and, if we are lucky, even lessen some of their difficulties.

This study builds on a continuous body of research extending over a 10-year period at the Institute for Research on Poverty of the University of Wisconsin. I owe a great debt to the institute for its intellectual and financial support, and to my principal collaborator and colleague, Ellen Jane Hollingsworth. Jerry Turem, Betsy Ginsberg, and Jeffrey Jowell read the entire manuscript and offered valuable suggestions for improvement. Robert Salinger assisted in research. Violette Moore was the incomparable typist.

I

The Issues:
Discretion and
Due Process Protection

1

Discretion in Social Services

THE LEGAL DIMENSION

Public social service agencies are created by statutes that prescribe their duties. The agencies allocate public money to provide goods and services, and they exercise the power of the state over the citizens who deal with them. They are like other public bureaucracies, such as hospitals, the police, schools, and prisons, which operate according to rules, standards, and funds structured by the legal system.

Private social service agencies are also clothed with law. As part of the voluntary sector, they are supported by laws that define their charters; they may receive public subsidies either through the tax system or by means of direct grants; their staffs are often licensed by state law; and their operations are bounded by the criminal law, by civil rights statutes, and by employment, health, and safety rules.

Despite this heavy overlay of law, the legal system took little notice of the operation of social services until the 1960s, when it came to light that in the course of administering public assistance programs various social welfare departments were intruding extensively into the lives of their clients. This was the period of the War on Poverty and the growth in legal rights for the poor. At first, attention was focused on the administration of the Aid to Families with Dependent Children (AFDC) program. It was found that attempts often were made to impose standards of moral behavior on recipients. For example, in Louisiana, aid to needy families was cut off if the mother gave birth to an illegitimate child while on relief, unless she could prove that she no longer had "illicit" relationships. Some departments threatened neglect proceedings against applicants with illegitimate children, and there were various man-in-the-house rules, enforced by surprise midnight raids without warrants, which resulted in either loss of eligibility or in a reduction in payment. Other invasions of privacy involved inquiries made in the community among merchants, employers, and relatives of clients to check financial eligibility and need. Every state promulgated work tests as well. In New York, men were required to cut brush in deep snow, under threat of criminal prosecution, in order to receive their relief checks; in areas of the South and the Northwest, welfare checks were stopped when crops ripened, and whole families were required to go into the fields. However, the AFDC program was not unique in this regard. Public housing authorities, for example, under their power to select tenants with certain financial qualifications, used impressions from interviews, police records, and information on the kind of company the family kept or whether they engaged in what the officials considered immoral conduct to exclude so-called undesirable tenants.[1]

According to workers for the legal rights of the poor, the problem with welfare administration was not only the outrageous practices of some of the more extreme departments, but also the fact that so much of the administration was bounded by vague, irrelevant, discretionary criteria. The gravamen of the charges against welfare administration in the 1960s was that many state and local practices violated both the Constitution and federal statutory law and subjected clients to unnecessary discretionary judgments that had little or no relationship to the purposes of the various social welfare programs. Why should an otherwise qualified applicant be denied public housing because a member of the family had a police record? And by what right did the housing manager have the authority to judge the character and moral behavior of the family? If the United States Constitution protects the ordinary citizen from warrantless searches by the

---

[1]See Reich (1963, 1965) for descriptions of the practices of public housing authorities and for citations to numerous sources. On welfare abuses, see the extensive compilations in *The Poverty Law Reporter*, the *Commerce Clearinghouse*, and the *Clearinghouse Review* for the last 10 years.

police, why were husbandless families not similarly protected from the midnight raids of welfare investigators? The problem was aggravated by social service plans, developed in the 1960s, that aimed at rehabilitating and reducing dependency among AFDC families (Handler and Rosenheim, 1966). The statutory language of these plans was vague: What did "rehabilitate" mean? Were the programs mandatory in the sense that refusing casework services meant that aid would be cut off? What particular services were subsumed under the term "social work services"? These rehabilitation requirements looked suspiciously like an additional overlay of conditions attached to the welfare grant. In addition to administrative requirements based on financial, moral, and employment standing, it now appeared that welfare applicants and grantees would be subject to psychological and family therapy controls as well.

Conditions attached to receipt of public assistance were, of course, not new. Relief for the poor has always been conditional.[2] What was new, however, was the changing conception of the legal nature of relief; it was now considered part of the "new property," a term popularized by Charles Reich in an article published in 1964. Reich's thesis was that because of the growth of government largess in the form of programs and benefits, new and extensive dependency relationships have been established between the citizen and the government and that, as a result, new legal protections have been fashioned to protect the citizen from arbitrary and capricious government power. Expanded government largess has taken a number of forms: income and benefits (Social Security, Unemployment Compensation, veterans' benefits, AFDC, state and local welfare); direct government employment; occupational licensing; franchises (ranging from TV stations to taxi cabs); government contracts; subsidies to agriculture, the airlines, and shipping; and government services (the post office, sewer systems, police and fire departments, home and bank insurance, and technical information). The range of government benefits and services is enormous and growing steadily. It creates extensive dependencies, many of them no longer voluntary, and these dependencies will increase as the welfare state expands.

Under traditional property law, government largess was considered a gratuity rather than a property right, and because the citizen was free to accept or reject the government offer, the government was free to impose whatever conditions it saw fit on the grant or contract. This traditional view

---

[2]For a history of the conditions of relief and other constraints on the poor from a legal perspective, see Handler (1964).

was rapidly eroded when business and occupational interests were at stake. Through statutory law and judicial interpretations of the Constitution, limitations were placed on the conditions that government could impose on the exercise of its largess, especially after expectancies had been established. Business investments and professional licenses could not be destroyed except according to previously announced legal standards, and procedural due process requirements of notice and opportunity to be heard were essential. Protection against government conditions and discretionary administration was extended under other theories of law. One such theory was that if the government did act, then it was bound by the Constitution and statutory law; thus, the government had no obligation to make a public auditorium available for private groups, but if it did, it could not insist that a group sign a loyalty oath.[3] Another theory was that certain privileges became, in effect, necessities and that a citizen would be seriously inconvenienced if denied the privilege—for example, a driver's license (Reich, 1964, pp. 741–742).

Reich argued that the erosion of the traditional distinction between property and gratuity was a recognition of the development of a new form of property, government largess, and that new forms of protections were needed to guard the rights of citizens in their dependency relations with government. To a considerable extent, these protections had been granted to businesses, commercial interests, and occupations. However, they had also to be extended to other forms of government benefits, such as Unemployment Compensation, welfare, health care, and the other programs affecting the poor. In two separate articles, Reich (1963, 1965) extended his analysis specifically to public assistance. He argued that the Constitution applied to welfare largess and that welfare administration abuses were illegal.

Along with the idea of the new property, there developed an expansive view of the Equal Protection Clause of the Fourteenth Amendment. For over 20 years, Jacobus tenBroek had argued that the conditions of relief had amounted to a dual system of law, a law for the rich and a law for the poor, and that this constituted an arbitrary and unreasonable classification

---

[3]See *Danskin* v. *San Diego Unified School District*, 28 Cal.2d 536, 171 P.2d 885 (1946), where the court said: "The state is under no duty to make school buildings available for public meetings. . . . If it elects to do so, however, it cannot arbitrarily prevent any members of the public from holding such meetings. . . ." For a full development of this legal theory, see O'Neil (1970).

in violation of the Equal Protection Clause (tenBroek and Tussman, 1949). The United States Supreme Court, under the leadership of Chief Justice Earl Warren, first used the Equal Protection Clause to outlaw school segregation in 1954 and later used it in a series of decisions attacking racial discrimination in other areas.[4] As a result of various federal judicial opinions and the influence of the civil rights movement of the late 1950s and early 1960s, the idea took hold that the poor were also discriminated against. Welfare rights activists insisted that the poor be treated in the same manner as the nonpoor, and that the moral behavior, family life, and parent–child relationships of the poor were no more the business of government than was the life style of the nonpoor. The activists resisted the notion that welfare applicants should be subjected to an investigation of eligibility and demanded that applicants be accorded equal treatment with taxpayers, that is, that the only requirement be a self-declaration of eligibility with random audits. They questioned the reasons for needy families to be subjected to social work rehabilitation plans as the price of survival, when nonpoor families were not required to undergo similar investigations. There was a rejection of the old idea that the poor were different from the rest of society in favor of the concept that they were just like everyone else except for the fact that, for various reasons most of which were beyond their control, they lacked financial resources. Consequently, it was argued that the only valid purpose of a public social welfare policy was to supply needed resources with a minimum of conditions and government interference in the lives of the poor.

From the perspective of legal rights advocates, the single most important problem presented by all public agencies, including social services, can be summed up in the word *discretion*.[5] Discretion is the opposite of fixed, clearly defined, and precisely stated eligibility rules and conditions. Discretion gives officials choices. In the context of this book, it refers specifically to the conditions imposed by social workers upon the recipients of social services. Discretion, however, is a matter of degree that manifests itself under varying circumstances. In some programs, rules are clear-cut and the choices allowed officials are minimal. However, such programs are

---

[4]*Brown* v. *Board of Education of Topeka, Kansas,* 347 U.S. 483 (1954); *Loving* v. *Virginia,* 388 U.S. 1 (1967) (miscegenation statutes); *Alexander* v. *Louisiana,* 405 U.S. 625 (1972) (jury selection).

[5]For a full discussion of the problems of discretion from a legal perspective, see Davis (1969) and Jowell (1975).

relatively rare. In most programs, and especially in the social service programs, officials are allowed great latitude in imposing conditions as part of the price for the delivery of social services.

Understanding and controlling official discretion is the key legal issue in social services. The law is concerned with how social service agencies exercise their discretion and, more particularly, with how the interests and rights of social service recipients are protected.

Although this book is written from a lawyer's perspective and thus reflects a lawyer's concern for the protection of client rights in social services, it is important to remember that different professions' views of the nature of discretion vary considerably. Poverty lawyers are appalled at what they perceive as the vague discretionary powers that social service officials appear to have over the lives of their clients, while social workers do not view their powers in that light. Discretion is inherent in all professional work, including the law, and many social workers consider themselves hemmed in by too many rules and otherwise inadequately empowered to do the jobs that they are supposed to do. They become frustrated and retire from public agencies, or they become jaded and perform their tasks routinely. The danger, in their view, is not from too much discretionary power but from too little. While I recognize that each profession has its own point of view, the discussion that follows attempts to reconcile the often conflicting requirements of social service agencies and the interests of social service clients.

Administrative or official discretion is a complex phenomenon. It arises from several sources and manifests itself in varying ways depending on its legal and structural context. In the remaining sections of this chapter, four principal sources of discretion are discussed.

SOURCES OF ADMINISTRATIVE DISCRETION

Positive Law: Statutes, Administrative Rules, and Guidelines

Administrative discretion begins with the enabling legislation, that is, the basic statutes that establish a given program and authorize the exercise of power. If the statute establishes fixed, clearly defined criteria for the exercise of agency choices, then discretion is narrowed. In the social services programs discussed here, statutory criteria are vague, ill-defined, ambiguous, and subject to conflicting and competing interpretations; the statutes are replete with phrases such as "achieving or maintaining self-sufficiency," "preserving, rehabilitating or reuniting families," "preventing or reducing inappropriate institutional care," and "reduction or prevention of dependency."[6] Vague language in the statutes, the administrative rules, or the guidelines creates a "downward flow" of discretion, which operates as follows. Initially, the supervising agency interprets the statutory language and issues its interpretations in the form of regulations. The drafting and promulgating of such regulations is an exercise of discretion; the agency is making interpretive choices. Not unexpectedly, the regulations are also often vague, so lower-level officials in turn have to make choices as to the meaning of the regulations. The process continues down through the administrative structure, until the lowest field officer interprets rules and guidelines for specific cases.

Regulating this downward flow of substantial amounts of discretion is of critical importance in the attempt to control the exercise of discretion. Because the use and abuse of discretion is one of the most serious issues facing the legal system, the first step in controlling discretion is to examine more closely why it is created in the first place. What are the reasons for legislative delegation of authority to administrative agencies, most especially to social services?

The principal reasons for legislative ambiguity and the consequent delegation of discretion to administrative agencies are lack of knowledge, lack of agreement on competing values, and the desire to have agencies develop consistent programs that require professional, technical, or other expert skills. Quite often legislatures are confronted with problems requiring some solution, but there is a lack of information as to how best to solve the problem. In these situations, the legislature defines the problem in general terms and delegates the task of finding solutions to an administrative agency. In other situations, there may be defined solutions to problems but the legislature is unable to agree on which solution to adopt. Faced with pressure to act, but unable to agree on what to do, the legislature turns to a favorite compromise—delegating the conflict to the administrative agency. In a third situation, the legislature is institutionally not suited to apply continuous expertise to a problem. The classic example here is rate regulation in transportation and public utilities.

All three of these reasons for statutory ambiguity and consequent delegation were present in the development of social services programs from

---

[6]Social Security Act, Title XX, s. 2001.

the 1950s through 1975, when Title XX of the Social Security law was enacted. About 20 years ago, social services programs began to emerge as a strategy to alleviate the various problems of poverty. During this time period, particular points of view gained partial dominance and alternative programs were always present. Throughout the debates and legislative changes, there was not only lack of agreement on the best course to pursue but also lack of information about what would work. The estimation of the need for continuous expert administration ebbed and flowed with changing perceptions of the problems and hoped-for solutions. The professional and ideological debates surrounding the legislative positions were subsequently reflected in the characteristics of the discretion delegated to the social services program.

The development of federally supported social services is intimately tied to the growth of AFDC. A dominant motif in congressional support for social services was the idea that somehow it would help solve the "welfare mess." Thus, a large part of the particular shape and content of social services can be explained by congressional perceptions of what the welfare mess consisted of at a particular time, and what social services could do about it. However, congressional perceptions tell only part of the story; state governments, the social work profession, and academics of both liberal and conservative stripe have also pressed strong views about social services that have shaped legislation and programs.

During the 1950s, when America discovered poverty, when costs rose, and when the racial and socioeconomic composition of the recipient population changed, AFDC started on its crisis journey. During this period, when the number of persons receiving aid increased, one of the early influences on what to do about poverty from a social services perspective came from a private consulting group called Community Research Associates (CRA). CRA attempted to measure the interrelatedness of dependency, ill health, maladjustment, and recreation need.[7] Its reports, based on empirical studies, brought to public attention the notion of the multiproblem family and the theory of a "vicious cycling of problems" established and perpetuated by the interaction of various types of problems in family function. CRA made two recommendations that had continuing significance for the future structure of social services programs. Because

---

[7]See Buell and Associates (1952, 1953, 1954a, 1954b) for a full discussion of the multiproblem family.

they found an interrelationship among several kinds of problems in families, CRA recommended the development of family rehabilitation programs to diagnose and treat all the problems of a single family. Second, public welfare departments were to be the central agency for the delivery and coordination of this rehabilitation service. Thus, CRA developed a theory of rehabilitation for multiproblem poor families and argued for a public program in the various welfare departments to implement that theory.

As Martin Rein (1970) pointed out, the CRA recommendations were picked up by what has been termed the "investment strategy" of the 1960s; in addition to the War on Poverty, there were various manpower programs and welfare policies designed to reduce dependency by emphasizing self-support. Social services took its place in the fight against poverty as an adjunct to welfare and other programs investing in human capital and began working with problem families to reduce what was then called "structural unemployment." Specifically, this meant that welfare families were to be rehabilitated through social services.

The first tentative steps toward this new role for social services were taken by the passage of the 1956 amendments to the Social Security Act, which authorized the creation of social services "to help maintain and strengthen family life and to help such parents or relatives to attain the maximum self-support and personal independence consistent with the maintenance of continuing parental care and protection."[8] This approach fit the current thinking in the social work profession. Despite some dissidents, profession spokesmen ridiculed the idea that money alone was sufficient to relieve the problems of welfare families, arguing for intensive counseling by highly skilled caseworkers handling small caseloads as the best method of rehabilitation.

Rehabilitation through social services received its biggest boost during the Kennedy administration when the Social Security Act was again amended in 1962. The 1962 amendments authorized the states to provide "rehabilitation and other services" to AFDC families, with an increase in federal cost sharing. Specifically, AFDC caseworkers were to define a family's "problem areas" and then to develop a "social service plan." The problem areas could include such things as unmarried parents and their

---

[8]Amendments to the Social Security Act, Title III, pt. 2, Public Law 880, 84th Cong., 1956. The history of these amendments is discussed in Handler (1973, pp. 117–123).

children, desertion or impending desertion, reduction in dependency, child protection, children with special problems, and problems in family functioning.

If a family had one or more of these problems (and it is hard to imagine an AFDC family that would not), the caseworker would develop a "social service plan" that entailed "the selection of steps to resolve the problem, or to help the client cope with it." Such a plan might include not only counseling but also helping the family obtain other services available in the community, such as medical care, child care, job training and placement, legal services, or referrals to other specialized agencies.

Because of financial incentives built into the legislation, the states responded swiftly to the 1962 amendments, but within 5 years Congress became disillusioned with the social-service-plan approach. Despite the claims of the proponents of the 1962 amendments, dependency on AFDC was not reduced, social services were still administered by untrained caseworkers, and the federal government had extreme difficulty in monitoring the program. No one was sure what the social service plans in fact meant, and it is probable that the states merely continued to do what they had previously done under AFDC—counsel clients on how to cope with the causes of their dependency.

By 1967 Congress decided that sterner measures than social services were needed to reduce dependency, and it established the Work Incentive Program (WIN). At about the same time, social work professionals were questioning the soundness of the marriage between welfare and social services. They called for a separation of the two, with social services still publicly financed but no longer tied to welfare and made available to larger segments of the population (see Hamilton, 1962; Morris, 1964; and Burns, 1965). Social services were continued in the 1967 amendments, but they were downgraded in importance. Instead, under WIN provisions, able-bodied AFDC family heads were required to work rather than merely to receive counseling. Social services, reflecting the new philosophy, were now work oriented. In the words of Mildred Rein (1975), "Personal competence . . . now became skills competence and was to lead less circuitously to work [p. 515]."

Despite this change in emphasis, the old goals of self-support and strengthening family life remained explicit in the 1967 amendments. To implement these goals, the states were required "to assist all appropriate persons to achieve employment and self-sufficiency, child care services, for persons required to accept work or training, foster care services, family planning services, protective services, services related to health needs, and services to meet particular needs of families and children." Moreover, these particular needs were defined to include education, homemaking, housing, reuniting families, money management, consumer education, child-rearing education, and protective and vendor payments (Rein, 1975, p. 518). There were two other important provisions in the 1967 amendments. The 1962 provision of services to welfare recipients was extended to potential users of services, and the welfare departments were authorized to purchase services from other agencies, including private agencies.

The significance of the 1967 amendments and of the HEW regulations was that despite the apparently clear intention of Congress to downgrade social services and to reorient them toward concrete (i.e., measurable) items and toward work, the language of the 1967 amendments was broad enough to cover practically any kind of service an agency wanted to provide. In addition, the amendments expanded the class of potential users and allowed the purchase of services from private as well as from public agencies. The statutory language and implementing regulations were so broad that field-level agencies could accept or reject, at their discretion, the congressional emphasis on work. In a review of the available empirical evidence, Mildred Rein (1975) has found that old ways persisted; in fact, very little of the new social service was work-oriented, and most of it pointed toward traditional social work concerns.

There were two other significant developments that grew out of the 1967 amendments. Starting about 1971, there was a tremendous growth in the amount of federal money spent on services, yet analysis showed that there was not a proportionate increase in services delivered to AFDC families. In fact, a national study showed a decline in services to AFDC families and a concomitant increase in social services expenditures for nonwelfare clients. The reason for this shift was that the states had found an enormous loophole in the Social Security Act, consisting of open-ended funding, loosely defined services, few restrictions on what money could be used for, the expansion of eligibility to include those eligible on a group basis, and permission to purchase services from other agencies. As a result, states began to "purchase" services from other state agencies. However, an HEW study found that most of these services had already been provided as state programs but that because of the 1967 amendments, the federal government would now pay for 75% of them. The second development was the enormous expansion of child care services, which comprised the second largest purchased item in 1972. Private purchase of services doubled between 1971 and 1972, and almost one-half came from private agencies (Rein, 1975).

The history of the 1967 amendments shows that despite Congress's rather clear-cut intentions to change the orientation of social services, HEW and the social work professionals, aided by state governments looking for federal funds, were able to use the statutory language to pursue traditional social work goals. As Mildred Rein points out, HEW was in a promotional mood during this period and, under the leadership of Wilbur Cohen, was interested in pursuing the growth of universal social services not tied to welfare. In this endeavor, Cohen was supported by the profession, by state government, and by private purchase agencies (Rein, 1975).

The next stage in the statutory development of social services policy did not result in legislation but is nevertheless important. In 1970, when Congress was debating the Family Assistance Act, the administration also sent to Congress a proposed Title XX, consisting of two parts, dealing with the reorganization of social services.[9] Part A dealt with the substance of social services in traditional terms; that is, to "strengthen family life and enhance family stability" and to "assist individuals to obtain or retain the capability for self-support or self-care." This part of Title XX was designed to reorient social services toward more specific objectives such as promoting child welfare and combatting dependency. But the new language also had another purpose—the expansion of public social services to include child welfare services that previously were handled by state child protection services. The new language was not accidental; one of the functions contemplated for social services under proposed Title XX was to prevent or remedy situations that resulted in the neglect, exploitation, or delinquency of children. This would have the effect of aligning social services more closely to the jurisdiction of juvenile courts. The other individual and family services that were provided for in Title XX were also specific services, such as referral and follow-up services, supportive services for manpower and employment programs, family and marriage counseling, and homemaker services.

Part B of proposed Title XX, entitled "Consolidated Health, Education, and Welfare Plans," would have begun the consolidation of local health, education, and welfare programs, with the goal of eventually establishing a comprehensive, integrated family service program, a subject that will be discussed in Chapter 6.

Title XX died along with the Family Assistance Act, but in 1972 Congress made another attempt at reforming social services. It put a ceiling on

---

[9]The Nixon proposals on Title XX are discussed in Handler (1973, pp. 127–132).

social services expenditures but allowed HEW to define both the specific social services goals and the requisite conditions for certain kinds of services. By 1972, the leadership of HEW had changed, and the agency proposed to restrict social services to the single goal of self-support, to sharply curtail available services, and to narrow the class of potential clients. The proposed regulations aroused vigorous and widespread opposition from those who sought to maintain the traditional goal of strengthening the family, extend services to nonwelfare or near-welfare populations, and provide a wide range of services. Significantly, the opposition was so strong that HEW capitulated, and the present Title XX was enacted as a result of an agreement among liberal senators, the National Governors' Conference, representatives of service agencies and other professional groups, and HEW (Rein, 1975, pp. 528–530).

The goals of Title XX adopt all three positions: (a) the hard-line congressional goal of "achieving or maintaining economic self-support to prevent, reduce, or eliminate dependency" and "achieving or maintaining self-sufficiency, including reduction or prevention of dependency"; (b) the proposed (1970) Title XX goal of "preventing or remedying neglect, abuse, or exploitation of children and adults unable to protect their own interests"; and (c) the traditional social work goal of "preserving, rehabilitating or reuniting families." Other goals include preventing or reducing "inappropriate institutional care," securing referral or admission to institutions, and providing institutional services.

Title XX provides a long list of examples of services, but the states are not restricted to this list; any service that can be shown to implement the statutory goals is eligible for federal matching funds. The class of potential clients is expanded, but one-half of the federal funding for services must go to welfare recipients. Individuals and families with incomes of up to 80% of the state median income can receive free services; those with incomes of 80 to 115% of the state median can receive partially subsidized services. Services can also be provided to those whose incomes are over 115% of the state median, but in such cases federal matching funds are not available. The private purchase of services is continued; thus the federal government will now subsidize voluntary sector services. There are also mechanisms for integration. The states are required to submit comprehensive service plans, and there is language in the statute calling for coordination with other federally funded human service programs.

Title XX thus represents a social services program that has broadly stated goals and that provides a wide range of services, both public and private, to the middle class as well as to the poor. The statutory structure, both in its substantive provisions for goals and authorized services and in its delivery mechanisms, creates a vast amount of discretion in the administration of social services. Programs at the state level can be restricted merely to developing economic self-sufficiency or can be broadened to include traditional therapeutic social work. Services can be tied to child protection services or to the state's education, health, or mental health systems. Programs can provide specific services, such as day care or meals-on-wheels, or more general ones, such as counseling. Delivery can be through public agencies or private purchasing agencies or both.

In reviewing the legislative history of Title XX it is easy to see why the statute does not resolve any of the policy issues involved in social services. The contending forces reached a standoff, and in order to get social services at all, Title XX had to include the goals and programs of all sides—the congressional faction interested in reducing dependency, the liberals and professionals who favored traditional goals, the state governments and private agencies seeking to preserve their financial stakes, and HEW, which by 1972 had shifted to a conservative position (Rein, 1975, p. 528). No one faction could prevail, so a legislative compromise was made; as a result, conflicts over the shape and content of specific social services programs were delegated to the administrative agencies, in this case HEW and the states.

The Bureaucratic Structure

Social services are administered through complex bureaucracies, which produce an increase of administrative discretion. Although organizational charts picture bureaucracies in pyramidal form with rules promulgated at the top and carried out through the chain of command, public agencies are massive, dense, complex organizations with enormous amounts of discretion that neither top management nor legislatures nor policymaking organs of government can control. Despite the fact that agencies are seldom given clear substantive goals to follow, the public expects them to be accountable to political leaders, to deal in an equitable and efficient manner with their clients, to be responsive to clients who fall outside of the rules, and to maintain fiscal integrity. Most of these goals are conflicting (see Hall, 1972, chap. 7; Wilson, 1973, chap. 3). Within the bureaucratic agencies themselves, there are often distinct and conflicting goals among individual administrators, among various agency departments, or among groups with different sources of information, attitudes, expertise, and perceptions. Conflicting goals make it difficult to measure performance or to persuade others to change their behavior. Superiors attempt to resolve conflicts among their lower-level personnel through bargaining, mediation, or adjudication rather than through commands. The bargaining process extends throughout the agency and includes relations between the organization's clients and its lower-level officials. Because lower-level officials have unique powers to control access to persons upon whom the agency is dependent, as well as information and physical resources, agencies "are, in a sense, continuously at the mercy of their lower participants [Mechanic, 1962, p. 349]." In study after study it has been demonstrated that field-level officials have the power to thwart high-level administrative decisions (see Prottas, 1978).

Social services bureaucracies have additional characteristics that further fragment the chain of command. One such factor is the decentralized nature of the federal—state—local—private structure. The conflicts between state welfare departments and HEW over the administration of AFDC are well known, and over the years state agencies have been particularly successful in resisting HEW's authority.[10] The history of the 1972 social services amendments shows that the AFDC pattern is also applicable to social services; the state bureaucracies with their allies in Congress, in the social work profession, and in the private sector were able to defeat HEW's attempt to restrict social services. The political power of state governments to resist HEW serves to increase state discretionary authority because of the lack of credibility in federal enforcement. State power is further increased by Title XX itself, which consciously decentralizes social services policy to the state level. The thrust of Title XX toward the states, combined with the traditional power of state governments, makes HEW control over social services programs even more tenuous.

The federal—state conflicts are repeated, more or less, at the state level when the state supervisory agency attempts to assert control over local public-service agencies and private purchasing agencies.[11] The legal power of a state government to withdraw or withhold funds is subject to the same constraints as is HEW's authority to withdraw funds from state govern-

---

[10]For a discussion of federal—state conflicts over welfare policy, see Handler (1972), Steiner (1966), and Rabin (1970).

[11]For a discussion of state—local conflicts in Wisconsin, see Handler and Goodstein (1968).

ment; the power is too drastic and thus, as a political matter, cannot be used.

The second distinctive character of social services that serves to increase administrative discretion is the nature of social service work itself. Simply stated, it is extremely difficult to monitor most social service activity (i.e., to obtain reliable information on decision making so that performance can be evaluated); and if activity is not readily susceptible to monitoring, then supervisory officials lack the necessary information to assert control. As Newman and Turem (1974) point out in "The Crisis of Accountability," outputs have to be measured objectively in order to evaluate performance, but social work goals are so generalized that they are not easily subject to measurement. The social work profession characteristically defines goals in terms of inputs (for example, the number of casework hours) rather than in terms of outputs. Goals such as reducing welfare rolls, strengthening family life, or eliminating juvenile delinquency cannot be measured in terms of what social workers are able to do with available resources. Presumably social services accomplish something, but they cannot be expected to effect major changes. Hence, the stress is on inputs, rather than on outputs. The principal social work method—more or less intensive casework—is difficult to monitor, primarily because the evaluator is not present at the counseling session and the reports from which the data are drawn are prepared by the social workers themselves. Thus, social workers are in a unique position to control information. One attempt to correct this situation involves quality control methods, but these are mostly restricted to evaluating objective matters, such as financial eligibility, in the case record. Quality control is far less effective in uncovering the personal, subtle interactions between client and caseworker that are presently so important in social services.

In sum, the bureaucratic structure is a source of discretion because the bureaucracy itself is a political arena where individuals and groups bargain and adjust competing interests and perceptions about goals and strategies and where rules are used as bargaining stakes rather than as commands. Discretion is increased, not confined, when groups bargain out their positions. This fragmentation is exacerbated by the four-tier decentralized structure in social services consisting of HEW and state, local, and private social service agencies. Discretion is also produced by the very nature of the social services bureaucracy; it is a system that limits the amount of information available to supervisors and controllers, thereby increasing the discretionary power of field-level personnel.

Professional Ideologies and Social Work Theory

The social services official, therefore, finds himself in a situation with a great deal of administrative discretion. In legal terminology, there is formal discretion created by vague statutory goals and by the multitude of available services; the social services worker is legally authorized to pick and choose among these services at his discretion. There is also the informal discretion created by the social system of the bureaucracy within which the social services official works. The crucial question is how do social services officials exercise both formal and informal discretion? The answer is that discretion is exercised according to social work theory.

The term *social work theory* sometimes causes difficulty. For example, it is sometimes claimed that there is no social work theory; rather, there is a social work "function" or social work "method." The term is used here to describe the structure of ideas that form the basis and guide for social work activities. All officials, especially when they operate in an area of wide discretion, make choices. To make those choices, they must have a way of looking at things, a set of assumptions to guide their activities and help them set their priorities. Such a conceptual framework underlies any system for the allocation of resources, and social service programs are no exception. This is what I mean by *social work theory*—the assumptions, concepts, and ideas that guide social workers in making choices.[12]

Traditional casework is the basic social work theory.[13] The foundation of American casework theory began with Mary Richmond's *Social Diagnosis,* published in 1917. Richmond viewed casework as individualized treatment, analogous to that provided by a doctor viewing the symptoms of a patient, discovering the underlying causes of those symptoms, and then prescribing a treatment. During the early twentieth century, social work was concerned with the poor and disadvantaged in society, and hence, looked at a broad range of social and economic problems, as well as at personal and family relationships.

In the 1920s, social work theory embraced psychiatry, and psychological problems replaced social and economic problems in importance. It was at this time that psychiatric social work developed into a specialty practiced primarily in an institutional setting or in private agencies or on a fee basis

---

[12]Compare this definition with Lukoff and Mencher (1962).
[13]See Handler (1973, pp. 6–9), Lubove (1965), Klein (1968), Mills (1949), and Hollis (1964) for discussion of traditional casework theory.

by private practitioners. The new practice arrangement and the new approach to client problems resulted in a shift of trained social workers away from serving the poor to serving the needs of the middle class. Professional social work remained outside the public sector serving the middle class until the 1956 and 1962 amendments.

Although casework recognizes both internal and external problems, external problems are downplayed. Although it is said that environmental factors can be determinative, the client's experiences and perceptions, according to theory, play the major role in shaping his situation. The caseworker has a duty to help ameliorate the environment, but the basic assumption is that the client "can almost always do something about his problem and that the worker's task is to increase his capacity to do so [Hollis, 1964, p. 17]." As Philip Klein, the author of *Philanthropy to Social Welfare* (1968), puts it, the aim of casework is to restore the individual's or the family's competence "to take command for reshaping . . . external limitations, or to effect personal changes in attitudes so as to 'do battle' with conditions as they are [p. 165]." The principal technique for improving client competence is relationship theory, which is comprised almost wholly of psychological concepts. Through a relationship with the caseworker, the client becomes motivated to achieve "adjustment, improvement, or rehabilitation." Caseworkers are advised to avoid meeting client's needs directly, but to help the client to bring about a change in the environment through the client's own efforts.[14]

There are a number of ways in which this social work theory—which in essence seeks reformation of the client—expands administrative discretion. First is the matter of intrusion into the lives of clients. By treating behavior merely as symptomatic of underlying problems, social work theory stresses the importance of penetrating below the surface to discover and then treat the underlying problem. But what are underlying problems and how far below the surface should the social worker probe? As with psychiatry, the stopping point is left to professional judgment. There are no objective measures of underlying problems or causes, and patients and clients are often in a poor position to judge when enough is enough.

The second reason why social work theory increases discretion is that, as in the monitoring of bureaucratic performance, results cannot be measured

---

[14]For an effort to combine concern with external as well as internal problems, see Gitterman and Germain (1976), "Needs and issues are reconceptualized from 'personality states' and 'environmental states' to problems in living [p. 602]."

either objectively or scientifically in most instances. We know from psychiatric case studies that it is virtually impossible to prove that a given result flowed from a particular kind of treatment. Empirical experiments are rare and complicated because there are too many confounding, uncontrollable variables. Thus, it is difficult to prove or disprove the effects of caseworker services on any particular client.

Even though the overwhelming majority of caseworkers in departments of welfare are not, technically, social workers (they lack the Master of Social Work [MSW] degree), social work theory still has an important influence on them. Field-level workers are directed by supervisors and administrators who usually are professional social workers. Social work theory is transmitted by these officials and by departmental manuals and is adopted by non-MSW staff.[15] Under Title XX, one would expect this influence to be even more pronounced because public social services departments, now separated from welfare assistance, will attract more professionals or more caseworkers interested in social work. In addition, a significant number of Title XX services will probably be delivered by private purchasing agencies staffed with higher proportions of professional social workers. If so, the importance of social work theory will be more pronounced.

Client Dependency

The fourth factor that creates administrative discretion is the client, who comes to the social services agency to obtain something of value. The client's need creates a dependency relationship that varies according to the characteristics of the client and the value of the goods or services desired.[16] Dependency relationships are easily visible among the poor. Not only do the poor have the welfare department to contend with, but, in addition, their children go to school, get into trouble with the law, and get sick. Adults also get into trouble, fall into debt, get cheated on purchases, and have difficulties with landlords. They need aid in getting help from a variety of public and private agencies. Social services departments have valuable things to offer—skilled referral and follow-up, advocacy, and counseling, as well as hard goods such as day care, homemaker services, transporta-

---

[15]See Handler and Hollingsworth (1971, pp. 49–55), where survey data show the adoption of professional ideologies by nonprofessional caseworkers.

[16]For earlier discussions of dependency in social welfare, see Handler (1973, pp. 136–137, and 1966) and O'Neil (1970).

tion and training services, protective services, and health support services. In short, to the extent that social services agencies have command over goods and services that people need and want, the agencies have power over clients; the agencies have discretion to grant or to deny aid, with or without conditions, and to decide not only who is eligible but what and how much is given.

Dependency, then, varies with how much the client values the benefits he receives and with the nature of the conditions that the officials are willing and able to impose. In the administration of social services in AFDC, it was found that when the clients were receiving "talking goods," that is, discussions and advice about social life, child care, or management of the home, they felt independent of the caseworkers and free to reject their advice; on the other hand, when clients received something of great value, for example, a Medicaid card, they felt very dependent and not free to reject caseworker advice. These findings were corroborated in a study of the Childrens' Departments in Great Britain, where it was found that the more valuable the good or service, the more dependent was the client (Handler and Hollingsworth, 1971, p. 5).[17] When social service officials become relevant to clients' lives by virtue of their power to dispense goods and services that clients really need and want, then the clients are less free to reject the services, and the power of the agencies is increased accordingly.

Social work theory comes into play at this point because it helps determine how an agency allocates its scarce resources. Goods and services are distributed to those who respond to the goals of the agency—the casework plan. This is a rational system of allocation; indeed, it is the reason for distributing goods and service through social work agencies.

Under Title XX, one-half of the social services are delegated by law to the poor. The eligibility criteria for the other half extend fairly high up the income ladder. Theoretically, one would expect dependency to lessen as clients become less poor; presumably they are less desperately in need of goods and services, and they should have more personal resources to call upon in bargaining with social service agencies over conditions of aid. It also has been predicted that more purchasing agencies would handle middle-class social services than lower-class services, and that there would be more "creaming" in these agencies. This increase in middle-class services would tend to make the purchasing agencies more dependent on the

---

[17]On services in Great Britain, see Handler (1973).

cooperation of their clients, thus reducing client dependency because the clients would know that the agencies need them just as much as they need the agencies.

I do not want to imply that dependency is solely a phenomenon of low-income groups. Dependency relationships arise in all social classes whenever officials or professionals have discretionary authority over things that other people need and want. On the other hand, I do think that dependency is more severe among lower social classes, especially among the welfare poor, and this greater dependency has important implications for the exercise of discretion.

In theory, the existence of discretion in the delivery of social services creates a bargaining relationship between the client and the social services officer. Discretion gives the officer the authority to make choices which are based, on the one hand, on the rules, standards, and guidelines of the program and on his professional judgment and expertise, and on the other hand, on the requests, information, reasons, and arguments of the client. The client attempts to persuade the officer that benefits or services should be granted and promises to abide by the conditions of the grant. There are constraints on the bargaining relationship. Both the client and the officer, at least in theory, are bound by the procedural and substantive rules of the program, and, as will be pointed out, remedies are available with which to enforce these constraints.

As will be shown in subsequent chapters, however, there exist in the bargaining relationship deficiencies created by discretion in social services. For a variety of reasons, clients lack the ability to bargain. They lack information about the programs and the applicable rules and remedies. They lack the skill with which to marshall support for their case, and they lack the power of exit. There are also more general problems commonly associated with people who suffer from a chronic lack of income. Their lack of bargaining ability serves to increase the leverage that social services officers already have. The officers are in a monopoly position, and they can withhold relevant information.

In other words, the imbalance of resources between clients and officers undermines the bargaining relationship because the officers hold too many cards. The clients are incapable not only of asserting their position but also of enforcing their legal rights. The powerlessness of the client is most dramatically illustrated in the hearing process, where the law attempts to equalize the bargaining positions by not only affording the client extensive procedural protections, but also by lodging decision-making authority in a disinterested hearing officer and by providing judicial review. The disjuncture between what the law attempts to provide in theory and what goes on in practice is huge. From the client's perspective, the constraints on official discretion are minimal.

DISCRETION AND LEGALITY

The existence of discretion has always created a tension in American law. Basic constitutional theory prescribes that valid laws can only emanate from the elected representatives of the sovereign people, yet the public business requires that lawmaking (discretion) be delegated to administrative agencies. Legislatures, as institutions, are simply not capable of nor suited for handling the day-to-day details of large, complex problems. But how, then, can this lawmaking by appointed officials be justified? The answer, in theory, is that although the legislature delegates lawmaking authority to agencies, it limits the discretion by rules and standards in the authorizing statutes that chart the parameters of agency discretion and establish the principles or guidelines for the exercise of the discretion. The courts are available to enforce the limits and guidelines set by the legislature. An aggrieved party (in this case, a social service client) can appeal an agency decision to the courts, and if the court finds that the agency decision conflicts with the legislation, corrective action will be ordered. The court will have found what the law calls "an abuse of discretion." Chapters 2 and 3 examine the utility of the remedy of appeal to the courts to correct agency discretion

This chapter has exploded the first myth. With social services, Congress created and delegated administrative discretion that is neither confined nor guided by rules or standards. Except for the most blatant and egregious forms of maladministration (for example, overt racial discrimination), the statutes fail to provide any boundaries or principles that can serve as guidelines for agency decisions. The parameters and standards that do exist are vague and ill-defined. Moreover, as we have seen, the formal, statutory discretion is expanded by other factors in the program—the bureaucratic structure, the nature of the social work task, and the social and economic conditions of the client. Discretionary authority is increased because legislators, policymakers, and supervisors have difficulty in finding out what is going on, in measuring performance, and in imposing sanctions. Clients lack the information and resources to bargain or risk challenges. In short, discretion exists at every point in the complex structure. As one moves from the enabling legislation through the three- or four-tiered bureaucracy to the caseworker-client interaction, informal discretion builds on the formal, legally delegated discretion. Discretion becomes cumulative and pervasive.

The existence of widespread discretion does not lead to the conclusion that administrative behavior is completely unfettered. In social services, as in other administrative systems, there are constraints. Despite wide grants of authority, state, local, and private agencies will pick and choose among programs; some will be funded, but not others. Also, there will be selections in eligibility rules and other conditions of aid. Administrators, supervisors, and caseworkers will also be constrained. They have professional and bureaucratic norms; they have their own sense of what is lawful and proper under the laws and regulations. In addition, the bargaining within and between agencies will constrain behavior. Discretion, then, is not boundless. However, the important point is that the constraints on discretion, for the most part, arise outside of the legal framework; they are not imposed by law and consequently will not serve as legal protections for aggrieved clients. If an agency chooses to fund a program in a particular way under particular conditions, these constraints are matters of administrative grace. Except for gross maladministration, the reviewing court will not correct agency decisions because there is nothing in the statutory framework that says what the agency is doing is out of bounds. A similar analysis applies to the caseworker decisions. Because there are no sharply defined conditions of aid or procedures for making decisions, constraints on these decisions are also self-imposed. Caseworkers and supervisors may treat clients kindly and wisely, or suspiciously and with hostility; they may view the law and the program liberally or restrictively, but in most cases, the law does not tell them which path to choose. Administration depends on the proclivities of the administrators, not on the boundaries and principles of a legal framework.

2

The Protection of
Individual Rights:
Legal Theory

Chapter 1 describes the discretionary authority inherent in the operation of social services agencies. The concern of the law is that this discretion be exercised according to the rules, standards, and policies of given social services programs, and that the individuals who deal with social services agencies are treated fairly. This chapter is concerned with those individual disputes in which an agency decides that a particular person is not entitled to a service and the person disagrees, or where the agency imposes conditions that the individual thinks are illegal. Such individual disputes must be distinguished from discretionary decisions that have a broader impact, as, for example, a decision by a state not to use Title XX money for a specific service or a decision that only certain services will be offered in particular areas of the states or a decision that different eligibility rules will apply in different parts of a state.

At the present time, it is unclear whether these broad policy issues can still be challenged in court. For a considerable time, federal courts were hospitable to class-action and test-case litigation that challenged many of these broad issues. Now, however, we are in a period of judicial retrenchment. Under the leadership of Chief Justice Warren Burger, the Supreme Court has cut back sharply on the number of individuals and groups who

27

have standing to bring lawsuits, and the Court has strongly intimated that it is now going to avoid balancing broad social policies.[1] For example, one of the principal reasons for requiring statewide uniformity in the delivery of social services was to prevent states from discriminating against minorities concentrated in particular geographic areas within the state. In the past, one would have guessed that if it could be shown that a state variation in eligibility requirements had the effect of denying a minority group a particular service, then the federal courts would have found the state rule unconstitutional. Such a result is now far from certain. In a recent decision, the Supreme Court refused to invalidate an employment test that, while neutral on its face, was discriminatory in impact.[2] Thus, the area of class-action and test-case litigation is in flux. Membership on the Supreme Court changes, and it may be that by the time challenges to Title XX reach the Court they will be received more hospitably. In any event, my concern is with individual disputes rather than with legal challenges to broad policy questions. This is not because I deny the value of test-case litigation, but because I believe that more attention and effort should be made to secure individual justice in the day-to-day, low-visibility decisions that confront ordinary people in their dealings with social services agencies.

Title XX provides that persons for whom services have been denied, reduced, or terminated or whose applications for service have not been acted upon with reasonable promptness have a right to a fair hearing, which is defined as an appeal to a higher administrative official to have the initial decision changed.[3] The right to a fair hearing originated in the Social Security Act of 1935, and was one of the conditions on which the federal government insisted in return for support of state categorical assistance programs. The jurisdiction that administers the assistance program—the states in the case of both AFDC and Title XX—also administers the fair hearing system pursuant to HEW regulations.[4]

The history of the fair hearing provisions reflects the history of the AFDC program. For a long time, fair hearings were seldom noticed and rarely used. Then, in the 1960s, these provisions became a principal organizing

---

[1]For standing decisions, see *Warth* v. *Seldin,* 422 U.S. 490 (1975) and *Simon* v. *Eastern Kentucky Welfare Rights Organization,* 426 U.S. 26. On substantive questions, see *Washington* v. *Davis,* 426 U.S. 29.
[2]*Washington* v. *Davis,* 96 S.Ct. at 2051.
[3]Social Security Act, Title XX, §2003(d) (1) (A).
[4]40 CFR §228.14; 45 CFR 205.10.

tool of the welfare rights movement.[5] It was during this period that several of the fair hearing provisions were tested in court, and as a result many important judicial opinions defining the necessary procedural requirements for a fair hearing were handed down. The conditions and terms of fair hearings, therefore, are not only a matter of federal and state statutes and regulations, but also of federal and state constitutional law.

During this time, fair hearings became embroiled in the social and political battles of welfare, and they also became controversial. It is claimed by some that there has been a vast increase in the number of welfare hearings and that many are needless and wasteful; on the other hand, it is also claimed that the system is still ineffective to protect client rights (Friendly, 1975; Baum, 1974; Mashaw, 1974). The controversy over the usefulness of fair hearings is reflected in the Title XX regulations, in which HEW noted that the states argued for the abandonment of the uniform federal fair hearing provisions as inapplicable to social services and to the differing needs of the states. Although the arguments against uniform federal standards were rejected, HEW proposed new fair hearing regulations which are discussed in Chapter 3.[6]

CONSTITUTIONAL DOCTRINE: THE APPLICABILITY OF THE DUE PROCESS CLAUSE TO FAIR HEARINGS[7]

Federal and state constitutions provide that no person shall be deprived of life, liberty, or property without due process of law. To what extent is this clause applicable to Title XX?

The application of the Due Process Clause to agency action involves a two-step analysis. The first question is whether the client has an interest protected by the Due Process Clause. If he does, the second question is what process is due, that is, what decision-making procedures are necessary to protect that interest. The classic model of the Due Process Clause is

---

[5]For an account of the development of fair hearings, see Cloward and Piven (1972) and Gellhorn (1967).

[6]Proposed new fair hearing regulations were submitted for public comment but then withdrawn (*Federal Register,* 1976).

[7]The analysis of the application of the Due Process Clause to administrative decision making follows, in general, the analysis and presentation of Friendly (1975).

the criminal trial. The interest involved is the liberty of the accused. The decision-making procedure is the formal, judicial criminal trial, which consists of the following essential due process elements: (a) timely and specific notice of the issues to be resolved at the hearing, that is, of the criminal charge; (b) the right of the accused to appear and to present evidence in his favor; (c) the right to be represented by counsel; (d) the right to confront and cross-examine opposing witnesses; (e) the right to a public trial; (f) the right to impartial decision makers, namely the court and the jury; (g) the right to a decision based exclusively on the evidence and arguments submitted at the hearing or otherwise made part of the record; and (h) the right to written findings of fact and conclusions of law. In direct contrast to this due process model is the managerial or executive decision, which is made unilaterally by the manager or executive with none of the trial-type procedures.[8]

The overwhelming majority of decisions made by government are of the managerial type, despite the fact that these are decisions that affect people's lives, liberty, and property. For the most part, the Due Process Clause does not apply to governmental decisions to declare war or impose taxes, or to many other decisions that affect the well-being of the citizenry. On the other hand, many governmental decisions are subject to the Due Process Clause. Whether or not the Due Process Clause is applicable to particular decisions is a complicated subject with a long judicial history. However, one part of the history relevant here is the distinction between rights and privileges.[9] If a person had no right to a particular relationship with government—for example, a contract or a job—then as far as the Constitution was concerned, the government could attach virtually whatever requirements it wanted to the relationship. Such a relationship was considered a privilege to which constitutional due process was irrelevant. The classic example of a privilege is a liquor license. Since it is illegal to sell liquor without a license, no one has a constitutional right to sell liquor. If the government chooses to grant a person a license to sell liquor, that person possesses only a privilege subject to whatever conditions the government may impose. One of the conditions is that the license can be summarily revoked—that is, it can be revoked without any trial-type procedures—and this method has been upheld by the courts.[10]

---

[8]For a useful discussion of the alternative models of decision making, see Boyer (1972).
[9]For a discussion of the "rights–privilege" distinction, see Van Alstyne (1968).
[10]*Smith* v. *Iowa Liquor Control Commission*, 169 N.W.2d 803 (1969). See Schwartz (1976) on this issue.

Until the 1960s, welfare, education, and other kinds of social benefits were classified as privileges not covered by the Due Process Clause. Over the years, as the concept of the "new property" emerged, the distinction between rights and privileges began to erode and the courts began to restrict the types of conditions that government could attach to important relationships. The watershed case was *Goldberg v. Kelly,* decided in 1970.[11] The issue was whether a welfare recipient was entitled to a fair hearing before, rather than after, her AFDC benefits were terminated. The first question confronting the court was whether the Due Process Clause applied to welfare benefits; if it did not, then the recipient would be entitled only to a posttermination hearing. In deciding that the Due Process Clause was applicable, the Supreme Court rejected the right–privilege distinction and said that the Constitution applied as much to welfare as it did to other forms of government benefits, such as Unemployment Compensation, tax exemptions, and public employment. Instead of trying to classify relationships in terms of rights or privileges, the Court held that the applicability of due process depended on balancing the nature of the injury alleged to have been suffered against the government interest in summary decision making. The Court spoke of the importance of the recipient's interest in the following terms:

> For qualified recipients, welfare provides the means to obtain essential food, clothing, housing and medical care. Thus the crucial factor in this context . . . is that termination of aid pending resolution of a controversy over eligibility may deprive an *eligible* recipient of the very means by which to live while he waits. Since he lacks independent resources, his situation becomes immediately desperate. His need to concentrate upon finding the means for daily subsistence, in turn, adversely affects his ability to seek redress from the welfare bureaucracy [397 U.S. 254 (1970) at 264].

In the Court's opinion, the government's interest in avoiding a pretermination hearing was not significantly outweighed by the eligible recipient's interest in receiving uninterrupted welfare benefits, and the requirement of a pretermination hearing would not unduly burden the government's interests in efficiency and economy.

It is important to understand the technical basis of the Court's opinion in *Goldberg.* The recipient's legal interest in receiving welfare is granted by statute (i.e., the Social Security Act which created AFDC); it is not found in

---

[11]397 U.S. 254 (1970).

the language of the Due Process Clause. The Due Process Clause grants certain kinds of procedural rights to protect the legal interests of life, liberty, and property, but the clause itself does not establish these substantive interests; they must be found either in other provisions of the Constitution or, as in this case, in statutes. In other words, a statute or constitutional provision must first grant a legal interest or right; only then does the Due Process Clause apply.

The principles of *Goldberg* were applied by the courts in subsequent decisions in which due process hearing rights were held to apply to the suspension of a driver's license and to the revocation of parole and proba-tion.[12] The Court held that a teacher could not be fired without a hearing if he had either de facto or de jure tenure, or if, even lacking tenure, the firing would impair his future employment prospects by damaging his reputa-tion.[13] In 1975 the Court stretched the Due Process Clause to its farthest point to cover a student's 10-day suspension from a public high school. In *Goss* v. *Lopez*,[14] the Court found that although there is no constitutional right to an education, Ohio law provided for education and, therefore, constitutional considerations do arise. In the language of the Court:

> Having chosen to extend the right to an education to people of appellees' class generally, Ohio may not withdraw that right on grounds of misconduct, absent fundamentally fair procedures to determine whether the misconduct has oc-curred. . . . That is, having been granted the right to an education by state statute, the students now had a property interest in not having that right ab-ridged in an arbitrary manner; at stake was damage to the students' standing with their fellow pupils and their teachers as well as interfere[nce] with later opportunities for higher education and employment [419 U.S. 565 (1975) at 574].

The school authorities took the position that due process applies only when the student suffers a "severe detriment or grievous loss," and that a 10-day suspension is not such a loss. The Court rejected this argument and held that it is the nature of the interest at stake (i.e., is it an interest in life, liberty, or property?), and not its weight, that is determinative of whether

---

[12]The driver's license case is *Bell* v. *Burson*, 402 U.S. 535 (1941); the parole and proba-tion cases are *Morrissey* v. *Brewer*, 408 U.S. 471 (1972), and *Gagnon* v. *Scarpelli*, 411 U.S. 778 (1973).

[13]*Perry* v. *Sindermann*, 408 U.S. 593 (1972); *Board of Regents* v. *Roth*, 408 U.S. 564 (1972).

[14]419 U.S. 565 (1975).

due process applies. The Court also said that "as long as a property deprivation is not *de minimis,* its gravity is irrelevant to... whether account must be taken of the Due Process Clause." The Court held that a 10-day suspension is not a *de minimis* property deprivation and therefore could not be imposed without due process safeguards.[15]

Despite the significant extension of due process in *Goss* v. *Lopez,* there are some situations where hearings are not required. The *Goss* Court itself recognized some limitations—hearings are not required before an emergency suspension, that is, where the presence of the student poses a continuing threat of disruption. Even in such a situation, however, a hearing must follow as shortly after the sanction as possible. There are also minimal or trivial violations of an interest that do not require a hearing, such as a less than 10-day suspension or small variations in welfare grants; however, at this point it is impossible to tell just where the line between a minimal and a serious deprivation is to be drawn.

In the line of cases from *Goldberg* to *Goss,* the Court looked at the applicable statute that granted legal rights and provided for some sort of remedy, and gave maximum value to the former and minimum value to the latter. Thus, in both cases, the Court found important substantive rights (AFDC, education), which required due process safeguards. In both *Goldberg* and *Goss,* the Court found that the statutory remedies were not sufficient. In 1976, however, the Court showed a reluctance to find protected interests. In *Bishop* v. *Wood,*[16] a nonprobationary policeman in Marion, North Carolina, was fired, and he claimed that he should have been granted a hearing prior to his dismissal. The Court held that the lack of hearing did not violate the Due Process Clause because the state statute pursuant to which the policeman was hired created only a contract at will, not a property interest subject to due process protections.

Because the Court's reasoning was unclear, it is difficult to determine the extent to which *Bishop* applies to Title XX. In the classic employment contract at will, an employee (for example, a teacher) is hired for a fixed term (say, a year) and at the end of that year can be discharged with no specified reason. Retention is solely in the discretion of the employer. If this were the situation in *Bishop,* then it would have little applicability to Title XX because social services are granted on the basis of eligibility conditions, which serve to qualify the discretion of the agency; that is, if eligibility is

---

[15]419 U.S. 565 (1975) at 575–576.
[16]426 U.S. 341; 96 S.Ct. 2074 (1976).

satisfied, the service is given and continues as long as the eligibility continues. In other words, substantive conditions that limit discretionary authority are placed on the benefit or the relationship. The analogy is to an employment contract where discharge can be only for cause; such a contract has been recognized as a property interest protected by the Due Process Clause. Therefore, social services, which cannot be terminated without cause (i.e., lack of eligibility), should also be property within the meaning of the Due Process Clause.

The difficulty with this argument is that the state statute in the *Bishop* case provided that a permanent employee could not be fired unless, after notice, he failed to perform up to the standard of the job classification, or "continue[d] to be negligent, inefficient, or unfit to perform his duties." On its face this statute reads like an employment contract where discharge can only be for cause, and the Court said that if this were the case the Due Process Clause would apply. However, according to the North Carolina courts, the policeman's contract was an employment contract at will. The courts reached this conclusion because the statute did not provide for any hearing after discharge; the employee was entitled only to notice of the discharge, of the reasons for it, and of the effective date, and then only if the employee requested such notice. Under the statute these were the only procedural steps that the employer was required to follow. The statute precluded judicial review and this, the state court held, created a contract at will. The Supreme Court, accepting North Carolina's construction of its own law, found no property interest. In other words—and this is the crucial point—the procedural remedies in the statute were found to define the nature of the substantive interest. This was precisely the approach that had been rejected in the *Goldberg—Goss* line of decisions, in which the Court focused on the substantive interest and refused to allow the statutory remedies to define the interest. Currently, under *Bishop,* the statutory remedies serve to qualify the substantive interest. The *Bishop* approach is very similar to the right—privilege distinction; if a government benefit or relationship is granted under certain conditions, then those conditions define the extent and nature of the right.[17]

Although *Bishop* casts serious doubts on the validity of the *Goldberg—Goss* line of cases, it would be a mistake to conclude that henceforth the Due Process Clause is inapplicable to Title XX. *Bishop* was decided by a five-to-four Court, and was an ambiguous opinion based on

[17]For a further discussion of *Bishop* v. *Wood,* see Rabin (1976).

ambiguous state law. It is by no means certain that the opinion will last, especially since the Court is closely divided on the issues. In addition, Title XX is federal law and, therefore, judicial deference to state law and state autonomy do not come into play. But most importantly, Title XX not only places substantive conditions, which qualify discretion, on social services but also provides for fair hearings; thus it is distinguishable from *Bishop* despite the interpretation of the case. While there is no doubt that the present Supreme Court is far less sympathetic to the Due Process Clause than were previous courts, it is premature to conclude that the *Goldberg–Goss* line has been overruled and that the clause has no applicability to Title XX.

If we assume, then, that the Due Process Clause is still applicable to Title XX, the question remains as to what process is due. That is, granted that a social services client has a property interest in the services he receives, what procedural steps must the government take before abridging that interest? The *Goldberg* Court specified a fairly detailed list of formal procedural requirements; *Goss,* on the other hand, required only "some kind of hearing" or some kind of rudimentary give-and-take before the authorities reached a decision. What court decision, or what combinations of procedural requirements, apply to in-between cases? The test is an uncertain and subjective one which balances the importance of the private interest to be protected, on the one hand, against the costs or burdens of providing the protecting procedure, on the other. The *Goldberg* Court, stressing the critical importance of welfare grants to recipients, required a high degree of procedural formality and dismissed claims of government cost. In *Dixon* v. *Alabama State Board of Education,*[18] a case involving students who were expelled from school, the Court said that prior to expulsion the students were entitled (a) to notice, including a specific statement of the charges and the applicable regulations; (b) to the names of witnesses or copies of school reports; (c) to an opportunity to appear before the Board of Education and present evidence; and (d) if the hearing were not before the Board, to access to the results of the hearing. On the other hand, in *Goss,* which involved only a 10-day suspension, the Court merely required that the school authorities give the student oral or written notice of the charges and an opportunity to present his side of the story. The student had no right to an impartial decision maker, to representation by counsel, to cross-examination, or to witnesses on his behalf. The Court

---

[18]294 F.2d 150 (5th Cir., 1961), cert. denied, 368 U.S. 930 (1961).

said that in view of the nature of the sanction, too much procedural formality would unduly burden the educational process and cost too much.

Finally, in its latest decision, *Board of Curators* v. *Horowitz,*[19] a case involving the dismissal of a medical student, the Court drew a sharp distinction between misconduct, where some form of confrontation was necessary to hear the student's version of the facts, and failure to maintain academic standards. Although the Court felt that the student in *Horowitz* was, in fact, given ample notice and opportunity to present her position, it refused to apply judicialized trial-type procedures to the review of academic decision making, stressing the subjective and "expert evaluation of cumulative information [that] is not readily adapted to the procedural tools of judicial or administrative decisionmaking [p. 11]." Given the vacillating line of decisions as well as the variety of social services decisions, it is hard to predict how much, if any, due process procedure courts will require for decisions to deny, reduce, or terminate social service benefits.

What, then, are the elements of a hearing, and when do they apply?

1. *Right to timely and specific notice.* In order for an individual to be able to prepare his case, he must be given timely and specific notice of the basis for the proposed action against him. Whether the notice has to be in writing and how long in advance of the proposed action he must be notified varies with the circumstances. In *Goss* v. *Lopez,* oral notice almost contemporaneous with the proposed action was deemed sufficient; on the other hand, written notice to a prisoner one hour before his hearing was deemed a denial of due process even though the prisoner had received oral notice three days previously. Written notice in a form that the person can understand and allowing a reasonable time to prepare is the norm; the government would have to show special circumstances in order to justify departures from this norm.

2. *Right to appear to present evidence and to argue one's position.* The *Goldberg* case held that there must be an opportunity for oral presentation of favorable evidence and that allowing only a written statement by the recipient is not sufficient due process. The Court stressed the potential lack of writing ability on the part of welfare recipients and also noted that factual matters in controversy are best explored through oral testimony. Oral presentation is the norm, but written presentation might be sufficient if the subject matter is relatively uncomplicated and if the client can sufficiently understand the case against him and present his arguments in written form.

---

[19]*Board of Curators* v. *Horowitz* 98 S.Ct. 948 (1978).

Oral argument would not be necessary for certain types of medical or scientific questions, or according to *Horowitz,* for professional evaluative judgments.

Generally speaking, the complainant will be allowed to call witnesses on his behalf, although the hearing officer does have authority to limit the number of witnesses and the scope of their testimony. Exceptions occur if the calling of witnesses might endanger state institutions or programs. For example, the Supreme Court has said that prison officials hearing disciplinary cases have the right to limit the calling of witnesses if there is need for swift punishment, if a risk of reprisal exists, or if allowing access to other prisoners for the purpose of collecting statements might be dangerous.[20] In *Goss,* the Court also said that the right to call witnesses is limited where the student is more interested in disruption than in documenting his case.

3. *Right to counsel.* The *Goldberg* Court stated that the welfare recipient must be represented by counsel, although, unlike a criminal defendant, the welfare complainant has no right to government-appointed counsel. Subsequently, the Court retreated from this position. Although there is no doubt that counsel can be helpful in many administrative hearings, the introduction of counsel into a case can increase the adversary nature and complexity of the proceeding, and, in many situations, reduce the usefulness of the hearings. In the prison disciplinary cases, the Court declined to grant the right even of retained counsel. If the matter was complex or the prisoner was otherwise incapable of presenting his defense, then, said the Court, he should be allowed the assistance of other prisoners or the prison staff. In the school cases, the right to counsel varies with the seriousness of the offense; most commentators favor counsel in major disciplinary cases. The lower federal courts are divided on this issue, and *Goss* allows considerable flexibility.

4. *Right to confrontation and cross-examination.* This is perhaps the most controversial element of the trial-type hearing. The right of confrontation and cross-examination is extolled in glowing terms; yet, in many instances, cross-examination is at best useless and has produced delay, confusion, and expense. Doubt concerning the value of cross-examination is especially pronounced when evidence is of a scientific nature; it is claimed that in such cases differences in opinion are better examined through the testimony of specialists, with the final decision made by panels of experts (Friendly, 1975, pp. 1284–1285).

---

[20] *Wolff* v. *McDonnell,* 418 U.S. 539 (1974).

There are other problems with allowing cross-examination. In the prison cases, the Court recognized the dangers of resentment and reprisals and the value of preserving anonymity, and held that the extent of cross-examination should be left to the discretion of the prison authorities. Similar arguments are also advanced in housing and school cases where, as in the prison cases, there are continuing relationships and witnesses fear disclosure of their identity. This position, however, conflicts with the basic democratic principle that the accused has a right to know the nature of the charges against him. Accordingly, courts have tried to strike a balance. In one case involving the dismissal of a teacher, the complaining students were allowed to remain anonymous as long as the charges against the teacher were sufficiently specific to allow a meaningful response; if this were not possible, then there had to be confrontation and cross-examination. In another case, involving the honesty and integrity of a government employee, the court was required to make a specific finding that the government established good cause for keeping the names of the witnesses secret.

    5. *Right to an open or public proceeding.* Although this guarantee is considered fundamental in a criminal trial, due process does not require an open proceeding in certain kinds of administrative hearings. Thus, closed hearings have been upheld in prison disciplinary cases and in student cases. But even if the hearings are closed to the public and the press, should friends or family be allowed to attend? Again, distinctions are made on the basis of the existence of continuing relationships or institutional considerations. The argument is that in welfare cases there seems to be no good reason why family, friends, or other interested parties should not be allowed to attend. In other situations, such as schools or housing, with potential problems of disruption, then access should be restricted.

    6. *Right to an impartial decision maker.* The question here is how much prior participation in the complainant's affairs constitutes impermissible bias; it would obviously be impractical always to require a decision maker who had no connection whatsoever with the agency. The *Goldberg* Court allowed a welfare official to act as decision maker even though he had some prior involvement in the case. The decision maker, however, could not be an official who had "participated in making the determination under review." The degree of separation of functions between prosecutor and judge, as in all of the previously discussed procedural elements of due process, involves a weighing of costs against benefits. In *Goss,* an impartial decision maker was not required for the "give-and-take" hearing, but even in cases involving more serious sanctions, formal separation may not be required. In *Withrow* v. *Larkin,*[21] a local board of medical examiners was

allowed both to prosecute and to decide whether a doctor's license should be revoked. Separate investigative and decision-making functions were not required, because, said the Court, the agency lacked the necessary resources, there was no presumption of official bias, and there were other methods of insuring a fair decision. In *Horowitz* the decision to dismiss was made by a faculty−student committee with review by school officials.

7. *Right to a decision based on the record and to written findings of fact and conclusions of law.* One check on the fairness of the decision maker is to require that the decision be based only on evidence produced at the hearing or otherwise made part of the record (and thus accessible to the parties involved). Evidence that the decision is based on the record is reflected in written findings of fact and conclusions of law, which can serve as the test of the accuracy and fairness of the decision. Other important functions are also served by this requirement. Written findings of fact and conclusions of law produce agency uniformity in decisions, make decisions more palatable to the losers, and are essential if judicial review is to occur.

8. *Timing of the hearing.* At what stage in the controversy is the complainant entitled to his hearing? The normal sequence of events is that a sanction is imposed and then the complainant or claimant requests the hearing. If the initial decision is reversed, then the sanction is lifted and the claimant is restored to the status quo, which includes the retroactive payment of benefits. If a job was lost, then the claimant is reemployed with back pay. In the *Goldberg* case, however, the Court said that the hearing had to be held before the imposition of the sanction, because cutting off welfare assistance is so serious a sanction that the recipients would lack the capacity to pursue their hearing rights.

Goss v. *Lopez* also required a presanction hearing even though the case presented a situation where the normal sequence would seemingly apply. The student is suspended, he appeals, and, if he prevails, he returns to school and the suspension is expunged from his record. Why, then, did the school have to conduct the hearing before the suspension? Even if the student prevailed, he would have lost 10 days of school, and he would have suffered the stigma of suspension.

In any event, whatever rights to presanction hearings may have been established by *Goldberg* and *Goss,* they were curtailed in the recent decision of *Mathews* v. *Eldridge.*[22] In the latter case, the claimant had been receiving disability payments for a back injury under the Social Security

---

[21] *Withrow* v. *Larkin,* 421 U.S. 35 (1975).

[22] *Mathews* v. *Eldridge,* 424 U.S. 319; 96 S.Ct. 893 (1976); see Mashaw (1976) for further information on the case.

Act. As required by law, the claimant was periodically reexamined until the doctors issued a report, which was affirmed by the disability board, that the injury was cured and that disability payments should stop. The claimant's request for a pretermination hearing was rejected by the Court. The Court distinguished *Goldberg* on the grounds that the need in *Mathews* was not as desperate as that in *Goldberg* because the claimant here could go on general relief pending the outcome of the case. Furthermore, the matter in dispute did not particularly lend itself to an oral hearing but could be more easily and more accurately decided through the submission of written expert opinions. No doubt the Court was also bothered by factors raised in the *Goldberg* dissent. There, it was argued that the effect of the *Goldberg* pretermination rule would be that all recipients, even when faced with a lawful termination, would automatically request a hearing that would give them two or three months' extra benefits, and, in view of the recipients' low incomes, it would be unlikely that the government could recover the overpayments. In *Mathews,* the Social Security Administration was faced with the same problem; claimants would contest termination and automatically receive an extra few months' benefits. In the post-*Goldberg* period, the number of welfare and Social Security hearings rose dramatically, and it may be that the Court was reluctant to provide an additional incentive for requesting a hearing.

As with the other elements of procedural due process, the time of the hearing will depend on a balancing of interests. The claimant will have to make a strong case of irreparable injury if benefits are discontinued pending the hearing. Suppose, for example, that authorities decide to remove a child from a special education program on the grounds that the child has not shown sufficient progress. If the parents can show that irreparable damage will occur—for example, that the child will retrogress or that the program will be filled and the child will thus be excluded—then the Court may order a presanction hearing. On the other hand, if the parents are seeking first-time entry for their child, it is doubtful whether a court would order a presanction hearing even though some of the same arguments might apply.

In sum, what does the Due Process Clause require in the way of governmental decision making? I have listed eight major elements of procedural due process, but there are no clear rules to determine which apply to a given situation, nor the extent to which any one applies. The law demands only that each situation requires a balancing of interests: (a) the seriousness of the sanction, against (b) the need for particular procedures to resolve questions accurately and fairly, against (c) the costs and burdens of such procedures. Although the Court has spoken strongly of the need to protect claimants' interests, it has also been mindful of administrative needs, and, in the cases before it, has tried to strike a balance. It has not imposed procedural rigidities.

JUDICIAL REVIEW: PROCEDURE AND SUBSTANCE

If a claimant loses at the administrative hearing level, he has a right to have the administrative decision reviewed by a court. In most instances, judicial review is limited in scope. A claimant usually cannot receive *de novo* or full review. Full review would mean relitigation of the entire issue as if the prior proceedings did not exist. In limited review the court examines the agency decision to see if any errors were committed. The reviewing court is restricted to the record produced at the administrative level; the court will not entertain the introduction of new evidence. If new evidence is produced that is deemed relevant to the case, the reviewing court will remand, that is, send the case back to the administrative level.

What is the scope of limited review? On what questions will the court substitute its judgment for that of the agency and on what questions will it defer to agency discretion? This is a difficult question to answer in the abstract, but the starting point is recognizing that the legislature has delegated the basic decision-making authority to the agencies. Agencies, not courts, are legislatively empowered to decide who should receive such services as welfare, disability benefits, special education, job placements, and health care. The substantive issues—who gets what and under what conditions—are committed by the legislature to agency discretion. On the other hand, agencies have to exercise their discretion according to law, and courts will review substantive decisions to see that the laws are not violated. Thus, to give an obvious example, social benefit agencies may not engage in racial discrimination in administering their programs.

Generally speaking, the extent to which a reviewing court will defer to agency discretion varies with the confidence the court has in the fairness of the agency's decision-making procedures and in the competence of the agency. If the procedures are fair in that the claimant has had a reasonable opportunity to present his case, and if it seems from the record that the agency has considered all of the evidence, then judicial review will be very limited. Under such circumstances, the court will not overturn the agency decision, even if the court would have decided the case the other way. If the court lacks confidence in the agency or finds the procedure faulty, the court will reverse the agency decision. Only rarely, however, will it directly enter a decision for the claimant on the merits—for example, grant the benefits. Usually, the court will remand to the agency for a redetermination in light of the rules specified by the court. Exceptions to remand occur where a redetermination by the agency would be meaningless—for example, when the sole ground for the claimant's lack of eligibility is a factor not permitted by law.

Suppose, for example, that a person's welfare payments were terminated on the grounds that she violated the work test. The recipient claims that the reason she refused the job was that the agency did not provide adequate day care although it is required to do so under the law. The agency claims that neighbors were available to take care of the recipient's children and that this constituted adequate day care. The question on review is whether neighborhood women constitute adequate day care within the meaning of the statute. There are at least three issues presented. First is the question, What does the statute mean by the term *day care?* Does it mean public day care centers, or private arrangements that are approved by public agencies, or both? This is a matter of statutory construction, or court interpretation of legislative intent. The court will not defer to agency discretion on a question of law such as this. If the court finds that some type of formal day care is required by statute, the case is ended; the recipient has not violated the work test and eligibility continues. Assuming, however, that care by neighbors is within the statutory requirement of "adequate day care," the next issue is, Who decides what is adequate, the recipient or the agency? Again, this is a matter of law for the exclusive decision of the court, based on statutory construction. If the court holds that the agency does have decision-making authority on the adequacy issue, the third issue arises: Was the particular day care arrangement in question adequate? This is a matter committed to agency discretion, and judicial review will be limited to a determination of whether there was an abuse of discretion, that is, whether the agency decision was so unreasonable as to indicate either prejudice or gross incompetence. Suppose, in our example, that the child was severely retarded and needed skilled care. Requiring the recipient to place the child with just an ordinary neighborhood woman who was also taking care of a number of other children would be unreasonable—an abuse of discretion. Reversals for abuse of discretion are rare, however. Unless the agency decision is patently outrageous, the most that a claimant can hope for is to challenge the agency on a procedural matter; in this situation, the court will remand the case to the agency for another hearing and will not enter substantive judgment for the claimant.[23]

The limited scope of review of substantive matters is very important under a statute such as Title XX. As noted in Chapter 1, social service agencies under Title XX have been granted extremely broad discretion. The goals of the statute range from the fairly narrow ones of economic self-sufficiency to the very broad one of rehabilitation. There is also very little statutory limit on the means that the agency can employ. The legislative history of Title XX and its predecessors shows that Congress made no choices as to either means or ends. Thus, a court would have difficulty finding almost any agency action to be substantively out of bounds. Agencies have discretion to distribute resources under very narrow or very broad conditions, and a court will not reverse an agency as long as the agency can show that its means (i.e., the conditions it imposes) are reasonably related to some valid statutory purpose. In short, under a statute as broad as Title XX, the test of reasonableness results in very limited substantive review.

LEGAL RIGHTS AND DISCRETION

The distinction between procedure and substance takes on added importance when one considers the nature of so-called legal rights to social benefits. In the discussion of the expansion of the Due Process Clause it was noted that the courts have expanded the number of interests—that is, rights—that are legally protectable under the Constitution and the governing statutes. The following discussion examines more closely what is meant by legal rights.

Statutes and court decisions speak in terms of legal rights, but in fact, a person has a legal right to social benefits only if his claim will be enforced in court.[24] Despite the label that the law attaches to a person's claim, it is not in fact a legal right if the claim is subject to a discretionary administrative decision. If an official has the discretion to decide whether to grant an interest, then the claimant does not have that interest. In order for a substantive legal right to exist, two conditions have to be satisfied: (a) eligibility has to be clear, and (b) the right has to be divisible. By divisible, I mean that the substantive interest does not have to be shared or rationed

---

[23]The scope of review in welfare is more fully discussed in Handler (1966).

[24]The following discussion of legal rights relies on the analysis of Friedman (1969).

among all the claimants who establish their legal right to that interest. If the interest is divisible, then each claimant will be able to receive his or her full share of that interest. Social Security Old Age and Survivors benefits, generally speaking, fulfill these two conditions. Once a person has accumulated a certain number of qualified quarters of employment, and other specific events have occurred (for example, death, attaining a certain age), then benefits are due. The benefits are monies paid by the U.S. government, and they are divisible. The eligible person thus has a legal right to Social Security benefits; if his claim is denied it will be enforced in court.

Suppose, however, the claim is for disability benefits. The benefits are divisible, but the conditions of eligibility may or may not be clear-cut. If physical disability is gross (for example, loss of a limb), discretion is minor, and the claimant has a legal right to the benefit. If such a claim is denied, the court will reverse for an abuse of discretion. If, however, the alleged disability is not gross but is subjective, as in the case of a nervous ailment or certain types of back injuries, the person does not have a legal right to benefit. The courts will defer to an administrative determination of whether the ailment qualifies for disability payments.

A third example involves rights to public housing. Here, eligibility may or may not be clear-cut (i.e., in addition to income eligibility, housing authorities may try to impose "suitability" criteria), but in any event, the interest is not divisible. There are only so many units of public housing available, and they have to be rationed. Therefore, even though the applicant satisfies the eligibility requirements, he does not necessarily get the apartment.

If eligibility is not clear-cut and/or the interest is not divisible, then what is the claimant entitled to? What are his legal rights? He is entitled to be treated fairly, and he has procedural rights—but not substantive rights. For example, if public housing is allocated on a first-come, first-served basis after the basic income eligibility criteria are established, the applicant has the right to be considered in order and the right to be placed on a waiting list but not the right to a unit held by another claimant.

This distinction between procedural and substantive legal rights is crucial to the delivery of social services under Title XX. A great many Title XX benefits are scarce (i.e., nondivisible), so no one has a legal right to any one item, although claimants do have the right to be treated fairly according to the agency's system of allocation. Furthermore, eligibility criteria, and especially the rules governing the system of allocation, are not clear-cut; in most instances services are not distributed on a first-come, first-served basis but depend upon recommendations made by the caseworker.

Thus there are, in fact, no legal rights to social services in the sense that once having established eligibility, a person has a legally enforceable right to a given service. Courts will defer to agency discretion, and claimants will be reduced to insisting on procedural fairness. In legal theory, then, the legal right to social services ultimately means only the right to be treated fairly, and not the right to a specific social service benefit. Legal rights under Title XX are largely a matter of procedural due process, and under the more recent Supreme Court rulings it is unclear how much process is due aggrieved social services clients.

3

The Protection of Individual Rights: Law in Action

CONSTRAINTS ON THE EXERCISE OF LEGAL RIGHTS

To this point, the discussion has centered on the legal standards and rules applicable to the exercise of governmental power in the administration of social benefits programs. These rules and standards are derived from statutes and from court decisions and are normative statements of how officials should exercise their power. They are not merely hortatory; they are commands backed by the full authority of the state. If a command is disobeyed and the case is brought before a court, the court will impose an authoritative sanction. The crucial question is the extent to which these normative commands are, in fact, obeyed. What are the conditions under which the system of procedural due process operates? How effective is the system in regulating official behavior and in protecting client interests?

There are a number of theoretical and empirical reasons for concluding that the due process system for clients in social benefit agencies is not functioning well. The due process system, or what lawyers call the adversary system, is a reactive system that begins to operate only when a complaint is lodged by a client or applicant of a social benefit system. The adversary system is based on the assumption that if officials err in providing services to citizens, then citizens will complain and invoke the due process system. Initiating a complaint involves filing a charge against an official and then proceeding toward the hearing described in Chapter 2. Evidence is presented, arguments are heard on both sides, and the matter is decided by an impartial decision maker. The adversary system presumes that the two sides will bring out the best evidence and arguments for their respective positions and that the truth will emerge as a result of the clash between opposing sides.

In order for this system to function, a number of conditions have to be satisfied: The potential complainant has to be aware of the fact that he has a legal right that has been violated; he has to be aware that a remedy is available; he has to have the resources with which to pursue the remedy; and he has to make a calculation that the expected benefits of pursuing the remedy outweigh the possible costs. Only if all of these conditions are fulfilled will the adversary system work. If any one of them is not fulfilled, there will not be a complaining client and the alleged deprivation of the legal right will not be challenged.

Meeting these conditions is especially difficult for lower-income people, who are the most likely to come into contact with social benefit agencies. Lower-income persons are often not aware of their legal rights or of available remedies. Once such a person is receiving benefits, he or she is most concerned with their continuation and is not eager to raise challenges or cause conflict. As empirical studies of AFDC recipients show, very few of the recipients were aware of the existence of a fair hearing system. It is probably true that many were simply uninformed, but it is also true that for many others, even though they were told about fair hearings at the time they applied for aid, it simply was not relevant information, and it slipped from memory. Whatever the reason, despite laws requiring recipients to be given information about rights and remedies and despite evidence that the information was probably given by officials, there was lack of knowledge on the part of the recipients.[1]

Assuming that the client knows about hearings, he then faces the resource problem. Resources include not only personal time and psychic energy, but also expert help, all of which are in short supply among lower-class people. Appeals, hearings, delays, and conferences are all costly in terms of money, energy, and time. There are problems of missing school or time at work and of making adequate day-care arrangements. There are numerous accounts of the difficulties that welfare recipients experience in

---

[1] Empirical results are reported in Handler (1969) and Mashaw (1971).

keeping appointments with school authorities, clinics, the welfare department, employment service offices, and social services agencies. These people simply do not have the ease of mobility that the more affluent enjoy.

Despite the great expansion of legal services over the years, the fact remains that compared to the need, the effort has been miserly; the overwhelming majority of poor and near-poor still lack adequate access to lawyers.[2] There has been some effort to train lay advocates to fill the void, but although some of these programs have been successful, on an overall basis very few recipient populations have been reached. Thus most poor people wishing to challenge government agencies must do it on their own.

The formal system is set up so that complaining clients are not required to have a lawyer, and procedures are relatively simple. For example, there is a minimum of formality in Social Security hearings. In AFDC, any kind of notice on the part of the client will start the hearing process, and the hearings themselves are conducted informally. From a lawyer's point of view the system looks simple and readily amenable to client self-help. In fact, from the client's perspective it looks and operates very differently. Bureaucrats do not have to wear a black robe and sit behind a raised desk in a dark paneled room to intimidate a poor person. We know from many different sources that the atmosphere of agency offices and hearing rooms can have an intimidating effect on complainants. And as we shall discuss shortly, the assembly-line processing of complainants does not put clients at ease.

It is also a mistake to think that because the government is not represented by counsel, the client suffers no disadvantage by self-help. The government representative in fair hearings is an institutional litigant—a skilled lay advocate who has been through many hearings. The complaining client is a one-time litigant without any prior training or experience and thus is at a great disadvantage.[3]

---

[2]See Handler, Hollingsworth, and Erlanger (1978) for a discussion of lawyers for the poor. In a recent empirical study of fair hearings in Wisconsin, clients were represented by lawyers in only 6.5% of all hearings, and the lawyers were only marginally useful (Hammer and Hartley, 1978).

[3]For a penetrating discussion on the comparative advantages and disadvantages of institutional litigants versus one-time litigants, see Galanter (1974). Again, the effects of this disparity are not speculative. Small claims courts were created to provide an informal hearing procedure where people with small claims could obtain justice on their own. In fact, most small claims have been converted into collection agencies for large institutional creditors. Their representatives constantly appear in these courts and have become very skilled in the system. The one-time debtor or creditor is at a serious disadvantage.

Assuming that the client can overcome all of the above hurdles, he then has to weigh the expected benefits against the expected costs. To a great extent, the calculus will depend on whether there is a continuing relationship between the parties. The complaining client, by definition, disagrees with the officer's decision, challenges that decision, appeals to the officer's superiors (i.e., the caseworker supervisor), prosecutes an appeal to a higher body, and, if successful, is vindicated by the higher body at the expense of all the other officials who have disagreed with him. In other words, a fair hearing is a serious challenge to the agency, a matter that is not taken lightly. If the stakes are high enough, the challenge will be taken. But one of the costs to be reckoned is that if the complaining client is in a continuing relationship with the agency, he may be subject to retaliation the next time the agency has discretionary decisions to make concerning his case. Often, actual reprisal is not the immediate issue, since the mere fear of reprisal has a chilling effect on the exercise of rights. The chilling effect on the continuing relationship is a well-documented phenomenon; moreover, it is applicable to all social classes.[4]

The range and scope of services available under Title XX serves to expand continuing relationships in two ways. The expanded array of benefits means that clients have to calculate whether a challenge today will diminish their chances of successfully applying for a different kind of benefit tomorrow. Families, especially poor families, have many needs that social services agencies can fulfill; thus, a continuing relationship is not necessarily dependent on membership in a specific program. Under Title XX, social services agencies also have an array of sanctions they can impose. Depending on the type of program they establish, agencies may have close connections with institutions and with child protection services, including the administration of juvenile justice. Thus, parents can be threatened with their own or their children's institutionalization, with removal of the children from the home, and with other coercive measures.

Under *Goldberg,* clients retained some leverage because sanctions could not be imposed prior to hearing. Now, under *Mathews* v. *Eldridge,* the leverage has been reversed; benefits are cut off and are restored only if the client prevails at the subsequent hearing. The denial of benefits pending the hearing makes the hearing less attractive because the client's resources, needed to pursue the remedy, are further diminished. Furthermore, because agencies have so many benefits to offer, the client is

---

[4]For a discussion of situations in which continuing relationships can discourage litigation, see Handler (1966).

more vulnerable to prehearing settlement, particularly if he has to come to the agency for additional benefits pending the disposition of his first case. Even if all of these hurdles have been overcome, the end of the road is still not necessarily in sight. The client has now prosecuted the appeal and has had the fair hearing. Let us also assume that the client has been able to present his case effectively, that the decision maker is not biased, and that the client has prevailed. Has the client won anything? This depends on the type of remedy sought. If the remedy is a one-time matter, for example, an increase in a rent allowance to permit the family to stay in a particular apartment, then the chances are that the client has won something. But if the matter requires continuing administrative discretion, we cannot be as confident. In the example of the welfare recipient who was charged with violating the work test by refusing the offered day care, let us assume that after she won in a fair hearing she was restored to welfare and the agency offered another day care arrangement. The new arrangement offers somewhat more skilled supervision than the first one provided, but the mother still thinks it is unsatisfactory. Her only recourse is to go through the entire hearing process again. As another example, let us assume a case where officials want to remove a child from a special education program for lack of progress or suitability. The parent is able to stop the removal through a fair hearing decision. In this type of case, the fair hearing decision has not ruled that the child is forever entitled to be in the program; it has only decided that the school program has not proved its case, and therefore is treating the child unfairly. The school can subsequently come back with new evidence and try to have the child removed again.

This brings us back to the original point about the difference between substantive and procedural rights. In most of these cases, the complaining client is entitled only to procedural fairness. The substance of what the client wants is a matter of agency discretion. As long as the agency treats the client fairly, the decision maker—whether fair hearing examiner or court—will not reverse the agency choice even though the decision maker might have reached a different decision independently. In the example of the working mother, once the day care reaches a threshold of skilled care, the hearing examiner or the court will affirm the agency. In the special education situation, as long as the school can show that there is a reasonable basis for its professional judgment (and the parents cannot show bias or the like), then the decision will stand. The continuing relationship is important, then, not only for subsequent discretionary decisions unrelated to the initial controversy, but also for the particular remedy being sought.

In addition to the constraints on the due process system from the perspective of the clients, there are bureaucratic constraints as well. As discussed in Chapter 1, the structure of the social welfare bureaucracy maximizes the downward flow of administrative discretion to the field level. Theoretically, one of the goals of the professional–client relationship is to maximize client self-determination. The professional social worker is supposed to lay out the options and advise his client on the consequences of various courses of action but at the same time to encourage the client to make his own decisions. According to the logic of this ideal, a fair hearing should be a prime opportunity for rehabilitation because the client stands on his own two feet and challenges the social worker and the agency.

In practice, the goal of client self-determination is rarely achieved. Client self-determination requires from the social worker time, patience, and a healthy respect for the client as a person. Unfortunately, these commodities are usually in short supply among practicing professionals, whose social class is usually different from that of their clients and who often lack understanding and sympathy for them. But even sympathetic professionals have difficulty in fulfilling the ideals of client self-determination. Many Office of Economic Opportunity (OEO) Legal Services lawyers, for example, were fully committed to client self-determination, and were sympathetic and respectful toward their clients as people, but found it difficult to muster the time and patience to fulfill the goals (*Yale Law Journal*, 1975). All experts, under the frustrations and pressures of heavy case loads, have a tendency to dictate to their clients. Moreover, as every practicing professional knows, when options are laid out for a client, he invariably asks what the professional thinks he ought to do. After all, this is what the expert is paid to do. The result is that client self-determination is often not practiced because professionals are busy or unsympathetic or feel that they really do know best anyway, and clients become confused and appear to want the professional to make the decisions, too.

Both the structure of the bureaucracy and the characteristics of professionals and of clients serve to enhance the discretion of field-level officials who are either professionals or who have adopted the norms of the profession. The fair hearing challenge is a direct affront to the field official's discretionary competence because the client first challenges the officer's decision, then asks the officer's supervisor to say that the client is right and the officer is wrong, and finally asks the hearing officer to say that the client is right and the whole agency is wrong. To add insult to injury, the hearing occurs outside the agency structure. In effect, then, the client is asking outsiders to evaluate the agency's professional judgment.

Finally, there are the internal costs of the fair hearing system. The field-level officers and the agency have to spend time and effort preparing for the hearing. They resent the fact that a client whom they think is both wrong and stubborn has the power to pull them away from their more important duties and require them to justify their decisions before a hearing examiner. Although there are enormous disparities in the due process system once the battle is joined, the system is a marvelous equalizer in forcing the strong and powerful to answer the charges of the small and weak. A welfare recipient does have the right to ask for a fair hearing, and the agency has to appear and defend itself even if it is the largest and most professional agency in the country.

Yet another due process constraint results from the nature of bureaucracies in general, and social services agencies in particular. The internal social system of such bureaucracies is rarely governed by rules. There is much discretion, and individuals and groups within the bureaucratic structure bargain and adjust competing interests. There have been many studies showing that lower-level subordinates have the capacity to ignore rules they disagree with (Mechanic, 1962). A fair hearing decision or court order is a rule emanating from authorities external to the bureaucracy, and there is no a priori reason to think that it will be treated differently from any other bureaucratic rule; in fact, a court order will most probably be viewed with more hostility and less legitimacy than are internal rules. Experienced administrative lawyers report that administrative agencies are notorious for ignoring court rules.[5] There are even further difficulties with enforcement under Title XX. Many of the services involve more than one bureaucracy; thus, blame for lack of compliance can be shifted from one agency to another. In addition, because of the nature of the work and the lack of monitoring and evaluation, it is difficult in many situations to prove or disprove compliance. A recalcitrant agency has the means to force the client into a difficult, long-term struggle to get enforcement of favorable decisions.

Another important constraint on the use of the due process system is that the system is not an automatic machine; it requires people to use it and to make it work. But the system's significant incentives run against making the system work. There is no payoff for the agency to encourage the use of fair hearings; indeed, the opposite is the case. Why should the agency facilitate the use of fair hearings? Why inform the clients of their rights? Why help and encourage clients to appeal? If clients are fearful of retaliation, why dispel that fear? The law, of course, commands the agency to inform clients of their rights and not to undermine the exercise of those

---

[5]Sources are collected in Handler (1966, p. 491).

rights by making threats, and it can be assumed that many agencies do not violate the law. On the other hand, as the next section shows, an examination of the empirical evidence on the due process system in a variety of contexts shows that the forces operating against the use of the system are powerful indeed.

FAIR HEARING PROCEDURES IN ACTION

Title XX mandates the states to provide for a system of fair hearings pursuant to which recipients or applicants may appeal a denial, reduction, or termination of a service, or the agency's failure to act upon a request for service. The Title XX regulations of HEW noted that several states argued that the current Social Security fair hearing regulations were not suitable for Title XX and stated that new provisions were being considered but that in the meantime the current regulations would apply. HEW rejected the position of the states that each state should be allowed to develop its own system of fair hearings; HEW insisted on a nationwide, uniform set of procedures. Although new regulations may eventually be promulgated, the chances are that they will resemble the current regulations in basic format. At any rate, it can be predicted that the major problems and difficulties encountered under the present system will still exist under the revised regulations. Therefore, the experience under the current fair hearing provisions is relevant to a study of the administration of Title XX.

The HEW regulations, which apply to all state and local categorical aid programs to which the federal government contributes, provide that whenever a state agency proposes to deny or modify benefits or fails to act upon an application promptly, the claimant is to be informed of his right to a hearing and how to obtain it. To be "timely," the notice must be mailed at least 10 days before the hearing. To be "adequate," the notice must state the intended agency action, the reasons for it, the regulations that support the action, the fact that the claimant may employ an attorney or other representative, and the fact that benefits will continue until the hearing is held. The hearing may be either before the state agency or at the local level with appeal to the state agency.[6]

A state may require that requests for hearings be in writing, but the HEW rules no longer mandate that states assist the claimant in preparing the

---

[6]45 CFR §206.10 (1975). For an analysis of HEW regulations, including recent changes, see Baum (1974, pp. 74–81).

request (even though a state may not "interfere" with the making of hearing requests). A hearing must be granted upon request, except in the case where state or federal law requires automatic grant adjustments for certain classes of recipients. Group hearings may be conducted if the sole issue is federal or state policy or changes in federal or state law. A request for a hearing may be dismissed or denied if withdrawn in writing, or if the claimant fails to appear at his scheduled hearing without good cause.

If the claimant loses at the initial evidentiary hearing, he has 15 days to request a state agency hearing and has the option of requesting a *de novo* or complete rehearing rather than a limited review of the record. In either event, a state need not continue aid after the initial adverse decision. The state fair hearing is to be conducted at a "reasonable" time, date, and place, before an impartial official or designee who was not directly involved in the initial determination of the action, and "adequate" preliminary written notice is to be given. The claimant has a right to examine the case file and other relevant documents, to retain an "authorized" representative, to present witnesses, advance arguments "without undue interference," question testimony, confront and cross-examine adverse witnesses, and establish all "pertinent" facts and circumstances. The decision is to be based solely on evidence and material produced at the hearing. The final decision is to be rendered in writing, within 90 days of the original request for a hearing. The claimant is to be notified of the decision in writing. If the decision is adverse, the notice is to inform the claimant of his right to appeal further. If the decision is favorable to the claimant, corrective retroactive payments are to be made.

The HEW regulations, which purport to implement the *Goldberg* decision, go beyond what is required by the Due Process Clause as subsequently interpreted by the Supreme Court. Clearly, there are many Title XX services whose loss the Court would consider less significant than the termination of AFDC and which therefore would require less procedural formality; but how much less, and for what kinds of services, is uncertain. Federal funds are disbursed only to states whose assistance plans conform to federal requirements. To qualify, the plan must provide for, among other things, an opportunity for all individuals to apply for assistance, the granting of aid to eligible persons with reasonable promptness, an opportunity for a fair hearing appeal before the state agency, and filing of periodic reports with the Secretary of HEW to assure compliance with federal requirements. After federal assistance is provided, the Secretary has authority to suspend federal payments if the state plan or its administration fails to comply with HEW standards.

In general, the state regulations are, on paper, in substantial compliance with the HEW rules and, in some instances, go further than HEW requires. For example, while HEW defines timely notice of a proposed action as a notice mailed 10 days before the action is to take effect, Wisconsin provides for 15 days' notice (State of Wisconsin, 1977, chap. 3, sec. B). And New York provides for fair hearings for objection to departmental policy, while HEW makes no mention of objections to policy as a basis for a hearing.[7] There are minor variations among the states, such as provisions for pretrial conferences, reimbursement for travel costs, and emphasis on helping clients prepare notices for a hearing, but none of these variations is significant in regard to implementing the basic *Goldberg* guarantees.

To date, a relatively small number of empirical studies dealing with the operation of AFDC fair hearings have been published. One study was done in Wisconsin in 1968.[8] Although this study predates *Goldberg v. Kelly,* the fair hearing requirements in Wisconsin at the time were in most respects similar to those mandated by the *Goldberg* court. The one major exception was that aid did not have to be continued until the time of the hearing. The study analyzed 449 AFDC appeal cases, which included all appeals in every second year from 1945 to 1965. In addition, state district supervisors were asked a series of questions about the fair hearing process. The study also included a survey of 766 AFDC recipients in Milwaukee and five other Wisconsin counties (two middle-sized and three rural) conducted during the summer and autumn of 1967 and focusing on recipient complaints and what the recipients did about them.

The statistical analysis of the cases showed very little use of the hearing system; only 1.2% of all denials of aid and only 0.4% of all terminations were ever appealed. Even within the small number of appeals, one could detect the chilling effects of the continuing relationship. Less than one-fourth of the appeals were challenges to changes in the grant; all of the other appeals were by persons who were off the program either because they were denied entry or because their aid was terminated.

The evidence also indicated that if an appeal was taken, clients fared rather well. During the time of the study, the state district supervisors, in addition to program development and supervision of county administration, took an active part in the fair hearing process. When an appeal was filed, the supervisor would immediately investigate the claim, and, in most

---

[7]17 NYCRR §§358.4(a)(b).
[8]See Handler (1969). This study has been updated, see Hammer and Hartley (1978).

cases, try to adjust the conflict. The supervisors looked at fair hearing appeals not only as a method of helping recipients but also as a means of detecting and correcting weaknesses in county administration. When supervisors were successful in adjusting the conflict, clients won in more than one-half of the cases; when the supervisors failed and the case went on to the hearing, clients lost more often. Combining both totals, however, clients won about half of the time.

Why, then, was the system so little used? Those supervisors who were older and who had been district supervisors for periods of from 10 to 30 years tended to have a more favorable opinion of the operation of the fair hearing process than did those who were younger and who had more recently left fieldwork. Most of the older group felt that clients were aware of the right to appeal, that few clients feared later reprisals from their caseworkers, and that the number of appeals was "about right." Most of the younger group painted a different picture; they were generally in agreement that there was an overall lack of knowledge among clients as to their right to appeal, that the presence of an ongoing relationship tended to reduce the number of appeals and that, overall, the appeal process was underutilized.

The survey of AFDC recipients themselves revealed a great lack of knowledge about the fair hearing system. When asked what they would do to change an unfair decision, only 2% mentioned an appeal. Although 31% had heard about the right to appeal, only one-fourth of that number knew how to go about it, that is, knew that they needed only to transmit some kind of oral or written message to the state office. Of those recipients who did have complaints against the agency, only 27% knew of the right to a fair hearing. This study was limited to recipients who had been on AFDC at least three months; either they had never been told about fair hearings or they had forgotten.[9]

The New York City Human Resources Administration (HRA) report on 411 fair hearings, held in October 1972, is the most extensive empirical study conducted since *Goldberg* v. *Kelly* (see Baum, 1974). The study was initiated at the request of the director of the United Welfare League, an organization which represents public assistance recipients at the hearings. It was conducted by six members of the city's Human Resources Administration Board of Evaluation. The evaluators observed each of the 411 hear-

---

[9]A follow-up study reached similar conclusions, namely, that overall there were very low levels of appeals and high rates of no-shows and that recipients lacked the information and resources necessary to cope with the hearing process (Hammer and Hartley, 1978).

ings, and each of the claimants was interviewed before and after the hearing. The record of each case was also examined to determine whether the regulatory requirements had been met.

Fair hearings in New York are held at the World Trade Center in lower Manhattan. An average of 58 hearings is held each day (approximately 10 per hearing examiner), and a majority of the hearings last less than 30 minutes. Waiting-room time was over 3 1/2 hours for over one-fourth of the appellants, and as a rule, waiting-room time for appellants with counsel tended to be longer than for those without counsel. Of the 411 hearings monitored, 52% of the original caseworker determinations were affirmed, 27% were reversed, and in 21% of the cases, the city withdrew its proposed action (resulting, in effect, in a "victory" for the client).

The study found that 21% of the time the notice given the claimant was not timely. In 24% of the cases, the notice given was considered adequate. However, in all cases a sufficient explanation of the claimant's right to representation and mention of the availability of legal services was not given on the notice form. Similarly, the notice form generally carried no written summary of documentary evidence of the action that the agency proposed to take; thus, even if the claimant received timely notice, he or she was not likely to know exactly what the hearing was to be about.

The agency record on the actual conduct of hearings was even poorer. In one-half of the cases, the person who made the original determination was not present at the hearing as required by agency regulations. No transcript was made in 22% of the hearings, and an opportunity to cross-examine adverse witnesses was afforded at only 2% of the hearings. Final decisions in 30% of the cases were not rendered within the required 60-day time limit, with the greatest time lag found in those cases where the agency's action was reversed. Cases where the claimant was represented by counsel also tended to be decided more slowly than those cases in which counsel was not present. It was also found that in 12% of the cases, claimants had their aid discontinued prior to the hearing in contravention of agency rules. The record on agency provision of resources to allow the claimant to pursue the hearing was also spotty; although 49% of claimants received reimbursement for transportation expenses when requested, only 29% apparently knew enough to make the request. None of the claimants requesting reimbursement for child care received it.

The report, after noting that many, if not most, of the state's fair hearing guidelines were not complied with, recommended (a) that the hearings be monitored for compliance with regulations at 6-month intervals; (b) that the Human Resources Administration establish an ombudsman service at the site of the fair hearings to act as a watchdog for appellants and to provide professional representation for appellants who desire it; (c) that city representatives receive thorough training in the procedural rights of clients before and during the hearing; (d) that city representatives withdraw the city's action when required procedures are not implemented; and (e) that steps be taken by city and state administrators to develop an efficient method for handling the daily calendar to minimize waiting time for appellants and their representatives.

The Virginia study, done in 1970, investigated two urban and three rural county welfare agencies (Mashaw, 1971). The researchers interviewed each member of the five local welfare boards, all departmental staff, and a sample of welfare recipients, including persons whose assistance had been terminated or who had been rejected after application for assistance. After a recipient was interviewed, his file was also reviewed for irregularities.

In interviews with welfare officials, it was found that most staff members "gave correct (i.e., consistent with the Virginia Manual of Policy and Procedure) answers to . . . inquiries about various aspects of the administration of their departments." Yet, the researchers continue:

> It is difficult to consider their answers anything more than reactions to hypothetical situations that they somehow do not meet in actual practice. We were told that the staff helps with appeals in a department that, according to state reports, has not had an appeal in more than a year. This department often fails to notify recipients either orally or in writing that they have a right to appeal when benefits are terminated. . . . Staff members purportedly give aid to applicants in filling out forms, "but not when they come in here in a welfare march." But the recipients report that their chances of getting an application form are very slim unless they approach the office in a group [pp. 830–831].

In one of the urban counties, the study showed that one-half of the rejected applicants interviewed were denied assistance because the department improperly computed need and income. None of these persons appealed. The situation was similar in rural areas. One applicant was rejected five times with no reason given, and another suffered three rejections for two different reasons, neither of which should have had any bearing on eligibility. In five of nine cases surveyed in another rural county, notices of denial or termination of assistance contained no explanation of the grounds for such action. Four cases were found in which a person completing a formal application received no response from the department, and applications in general were strongly discouraged.

> Discouragement of applications . . . takes a variety of forms: oral declarations of ineligibility ("before I can get in the door"), instructions to "come back some other time," statements that there is "no money," and "requests" that applica-

tions be withdrawn. The department visited one applicant at home three times
to "request" withdrawal until, feeling threatened, she did so [p. 835].

The results of these AFDC fair hearings studies show that a major problem is that the system is not often used. The nationwide appeal rate for
denials and terminations is only 6%, and three-fourths of those were
lodged in only four states—New York, California, Massachusetts, and
Texas (Baum, 1971, p. 50; Congressional Research Service, 1977, p.
164). It would appear that these low rates are caused by lack of information on appeal rights, inadequate notice, and pressures within the system
that deter appeals. When appeals are filed, the hearings are often conducted in an assembly-line fashion, waiting time is lengthy, there is little
cross-examination, claimants are not able to examine files beforehand, and
decisions are not rendered on time.[10]

Although there are many reasons for the failures of the fair hearing
system, structural factors should be emphasized. First, the system is adversary in nature; yet without adequate legal representation the recipient is in
no position to be an effective adversary. Recipients and applicants usually
are not informed by the agency of the availability of legal services and
generally cannot afford independent legal counsel. Second, the hearing
process does not act as a quality control system, since prior decisions on
appeal have little precedental value. Often, transcripts of hearings are not
made; nor is a narrative description of the factual basis for the decision
included, nor are decisions circulated to local officials. Third, the hearing
process does not produce information on patterns of problems in the
system. The hearing examiner does not launch an investigation to determine whether he is dealing with an isolated problem or with a widespread,
pervasive problem common to many recipients. Fourth, appeals do not act
as a supervisory check on initial determinations, since many reversals are
based on changed facts rather than on mistake. It is often hard to tell if a
reversal at the hearing is really a finding of error, or merely a natural result
of offering de novo hearings to dissatisfied claimants.[11]

To what extent are the findings on the AFDC experience relevant to fair
hearings under Title XX? The answer depends on several factors. In many
jurisdictions, Title XX may be administered in whole or in part by the same
public agencies that are presently administering the categorical aid programs, including AFDC, and therefore the expectation is that recipients of

---

[10]A smaller study of welfare appeals in Boston during 1967–1968 reached conclusions
similar to the studies discussed in text. See Jowell (1975).
[11]For a critical study of disability hearings, see Dixon (1973).

social services would have the same experience with the fair hearing system as did the AFDC recipients.

In larger jurisdictions, Title XX is administered by separate agencies, both public and private, but the AFDC fair hearings experience is still relevant. First, the state may choose to use one hearing system for all appeals under the Social Security Act. This is the present arrangement; the same fair hearing system decides not only AFDC cases but also Medicaid and Food Stamps cases and those arising from other federally assisted programs. Thus, Title XX cases are appealed through the regular, state-run fair hearing system, and Title XX recipients and applicants are in the queue along with everyone else and subject to the same deficiencies of the system. To the extent that hearings are held in inconvenient places, have long waiting times, are processed by assembly-line methods, and present other kinds of unpleasant barriers, Title XX clients will be discouraged from using them, as are AFDC recipients.

There are, however, significant differences between Title XX and AFDC. AFDC is a massive welfare program carrying with it all of the negative features commonly attributed to such programs. Title XX is a varied social services program, which offers a wide range of services to a broader spectrum of the population, including a more middle-class population, and is presumably administered by a more professional, better-trained staff, especially in the private agencies. Since a great deal of the difficulty with fair hearings is attributable to conditions existing before the hearing process begins—that is, to the caseworker–client relationship—one might expect that the differences in caseworker–client relationships under Title XX will affect the administration of fair hearings.

To date, there have been no studies of fair hearings in social services. On the other hand, there have been studies of hearings in special education, and the experience there will shed light on the problems that social services clients are likely to encounter.

In 1972 it was estimated that there were over 7 million children (or an estimated 10–12% of all children in the United States) with mental, physical, emotional, or learning handicaps that would require the provision of special education services at some point in their educational careers. It was also estimated that only 40% were receiving the education they needed and were entitled to receive under state and federal law (Kirk, 1962).[12]

[12]Other estimates range as high as 35% (see New York State Commission, 1972). The spread in figures is due to disparities in estimating the percentage of brain-injured and learning-disabled children.

The traditional method of dispensing special educational services has been for the schools to classify the handicapped by categorical labels, such as "trainable mentally retarded," and to provide services appropriate to the category. However, misclassification of children is a major problem and appears to be widespread. In Washington, D.C., for example, the school system concluded that up to two-thirds of its mildly handicapped students were in fact normal. Similarly, in a study of 36 school districts in the Philadelphia area, a change in testing indicated that two-thirds of the mildly retarded students were misclassified. Such misclassification can result in stereotyped expectations of behavior, in self-fulfilling prophesy, and in the deprivation of needed services (for example, a child classified as mentally retarded who also has a hearing impairment might be denied the attention of an agency providing speech and hearing services). Misjudgment may also result in the provision of special education services that are not needed (for example, many children with physical handicaps may not require special education, and may be harmed by the denial of normal school activities).[13]

Because of the seriousness of the problems associated with misplacements, there are now laws in some jurisdictions providing procedural safeguards before an intended placement occurs. The most legal activity has been in the areas of total denial of access to education and placement of children in categories to which their parents object. The legal reforms in three jurisdictions were reported in a study by Kirp et al. (1974).[14]

In Pennsylvania Association of Retarded Children (PARC) v. Commonwealth of Pennsylvania,[15] a three-judge federal court ratified a consent agreement assuring all retarded children the right to publicly supported education, and required that placement in classes for the handicapped be preceded by a formal due process hearing if the parent opposes the proposed assignment. The court implied that Pennsylvania's failure to offer any education to severely retarded children represented a denial of equal

---

[13]See Weintraub and Abeson (1972) and Hobsen v. Hansen, 269 F. Supp. 401, 490–91 (D.D.C., 1967). This reversal in judgment resulted from the substitution of individually administered I.Q. tests for group aptitude tests. For critiques of relying on group aptitude tests as a basis for student special education classification see Sarason (1959, pp. 482–487), Chase and Pugh (1971), and Heber (1961).

[14]Field research was conducted from November 1972 to April 1973. The researchers interviewed teachers, psychologists, special education administrators, and parents in five school districts, and officials in State Departments of Education. In addition, they observed special classes and admission committee meetings.

[15]343 F. Supp. 279 (E.D.Pa., 1972).

protection and that assignment of youngsters to programs for the retarded, unless preceded by notice and hearing, violated due process.

The formal due process requirements provided for in *PARC* assured the right to a hearing upon initial school placement, after any program change, and after every 2 years of special class assignment. Prior to the hearing, parents may examine school records. At the hearing, parents are entitled to retain counsel, demand that the hearing be either open or closed, and summon and question all school personnel involved in the decision.

Kirp *et al.* report that soon after the decree in *PARC* was handed down, 61 hearing officers were appointed; yet 4 months later, only 13 officers had been trained and were working. This delay caused a serious backlog and placed a heavy burden on the trained officers, all of whom were employed full-time elsewhere. By April 1973, 255 hearings had been applied for, 47 had been held, decisions had been reached in 43, and 69 of the requested hearings had been cancelled. In the 25 hearings open to the public, 13 upheld the school's decision and 12 were decided in favor of the parents. Parents represented by counsel were significantly more likely to win a favorable ruling: In 9 of 12 cases where a lawyer was present, the parents won; the parents won in only 4 of the 13 cases where a lawyer was not present.

Observing the hearings in action, Kirp *et al.* report that many of the hearing officers are confused about their role and that they improperly turn away some cases and do not fully explore the issues in others. No provision was made for hearing officers to read one another's decisions, and no one had access to the transcripts of closed hearings; thus there is no system of precedent to guide the decision maker. Parents challenging a placement have no way of knowing what sort of proof is appropriate or what procedural burdens they must surmount, and school officials are similarly confused.

Kirp *et al.* also report that in one district in northeastern Pennsylvania, parties to the hearings became so antagonistic that teachers throughout the district referred no more children for evaluation. Evaluation was required by the *PARC* decree and is necessary to set the due process mechanisms into action. From this, Kirp *et al.* (1974) conclude:

> This episode suggests that teachers may not understand the purposes of the due process hearings. More importantly, it means that hearings can be conducted in a manner that not only defeats the spirit of the decree, but also keeps children needing other kinds of help from receiving it. It is another example of the complex dynamics which must be taken into account in order successfully to implement the reform contemplated in PARC [p. 81].

Exhibiting general pessimism, the master appointed by the court in PARC to oversee the procedural system called the results so far "an array of facades," and stated "there isn't much new educationally in Pennsylvania, as an outcome of the case."

In *Mills* v. *Board of Education*,[16] U.S. District Court for the District of Columbia held that children excluded from school as "uneducable" were entitled to public education and that procedural protections must be provided to children prior to their placement in special programs. Unlike the *PARC* court, this court did not appoint a master to oversee implementation of the decree; the responsibility for developing and carrying out a plan to identify, evaluate, and provide suitable educational opportunities for previously excluded children was left entirely to the District.

Mills entitled every student whom the District or parent wishes placed in special education classes to a due process hearing. Parents are to be notified of the intended placement, informed of their right to object at a hearing, and told of their right to be represented by counsel or by nonschool professionals competent to evaluate the student's situation. The session is closed unless the parents request otherwise. The decision of the hearing examiner is to be based solely on evidence introduced at the hearing, and the burden of justifying the proposed placement is on the District.

Most of the hearings conducted so far have been closed, so information on the conduct of hearings is sketchy. Also, the court decree made no provisions, such as those in *PARC,* for data keeping or for reporting either to the court or to the public. The absence of such provisions further adds to the lack of empirical data available. Based on a small sample of observed hearings, Kirp *et al.* (1974) report that only 1 in 10 parents appeared with lawyers or professional help during 1972–1973. They also report that in 4 of the first 11 special education hearings, the school's recommendation was disapproved; in the other 7, either it was approved or the school bowed to the parents' preference. They add:

> District personnel have complained that one hearing officer "quibbled over terms," while another demonstrated "hostility" toward school personnel. Many of the hearings are conducted as conferences, with too little attention paid to the procedural formality which the *Mills* decree envisioned [pp. 94–95].

---

[16]348 F. Supp. 866 (D.D.C., 1972).

While the data on the operation of the *Mills* system provide a bleak picture, Kirp *et al.* believe that the system is improving. The number of requested hearings is increasing dramatically, and the District's 1974–1975 budget contained a substantial increase for special education programs. Yet they note that the District has "neither the resources nor the organizational commitment needed to translate that concern into substantial education reform [p. 96]."

The California system for insuring that students are properly placed in special education programs was imposed by the legislature rather than by the courts and differs markedly from the system of formal hearings employed in Pennsylvania and the District of Columbia. California's regulations require a thorough screening by an admissions committee of any child considered for special placement. Such screening is to include a developmental history of the child, a review of school experience, tests of academic achievement and aptitude, an appraisal of background factors which might affect a student's performance, a health study, and a statement by the school psychologist that the student is performing below reasonable expectation. Initial placement is followed by frequent reevaluations, an annual review, and a full case study once every 3 years. Before a child may be tested for placement, parental consent, preceded by an explanation of the reason for testing, must be secured. The parents may be represented by a professional before the admissions committee, but the representative's role is wholly advisory. Before the child can be actually placed in a special education class, parental consent is again required.[17]

The Kirp *et al.* examination of the California system found that the state requirements for placement "have become standard operating procedure." But they also found that actual decisions were made informally and that the formal process merely acted to ratify those decisions. They found that in some ghetto schools, students are never evaluated and just "wind up in the program." In a survey of 24 school districts, signed parental permission forms were on file for 79% of the pupils enrolled in special education, but this figure dropped to 55% in districts with high concentrations of black children. Often, permission from the parents is secured "without parents knowing what they are consenting to," since the permission form is but one of many documents the parents are asked to sign. And in the relatively rare instances of parental resistance, the reluctant parent

---

[17]Cal. Admin. Code tit. V §3231; Cal. Educ. Code §6902.085; §6755.2 (West 1973).

is barraged with evidence of his child's poor schoolwork as proof of the need
for special school attention. If that fails, school professionals can threaten to
leave a child back or, more distressingly for some parents, put the student on
reduced-day or home instruction [Kirp et al., p. 106].

The right to be professionally represented before the admissions committee is rarely exercised, usually because parents are unaware of it. And
once admitted to special programs, students often are not reevaluated as
required by law; the study found that 40% of special students had not been
evaluated since their placement.

These deviations from legislative requirements stem largely from the
absence of quality control measures. No steps have been taken to insure
that administrators follow the rules; hence, local administrators tailor requirements to their own purposes. As stated by Kirp et al., "to the extent
that standards promulgated by either branch of government seem imprac-
tical or unfeasible to school personnel, those standards may be ignored or
altered in operation [p. 113]."

In summary, the Kirp et al. study found that a change in legal standards
does not insure altered behavior by school officials. There are limitations
on what legislatures and courts can do to shape disputes, allocate resources, select among policy alternatives, and adjust rules to account for
changed circumstances. More importantly, both legislatures and courts
depend on state and local school officials to effectuate their mandates.
These factors limit any regulatory system seeking to significantly alter official behavior. Moreover, change becomes even more difficult when the
practices of more than one agency are called into question, as is typically
the case with respect to the severely handicapped, a group historically
excluded from schools and provided with minimal care by state welfare
agencies. The command that state welfare organizations coordinate their
activities raises many bureaucratic difficulties. The authors of the study
claim that "resistance to change does not [necessarily] result from the
obduracy of misguided school officials [p. 113]" but rather stems from the
fact that procedural reforms require significant reevaluation of structures
and organizational roles, which tends to threaten people in the system. To
achieve structural change, pressure stronger than the mere existence of a
legal requirement is required.

Compounding the difficulty of control is the fact that standards in special
education are not yet capable of specificity. Educators no longer have
confidence that I.Q. tests are an accurate method of determining special
education categories, but science has not yet evolved standards that can

empirically ascertain in what category a given child ought to be placed. Hence, placement decisions are necessarily subjective.

In this context, it is important to construct a mechanism to insure that children who are destined for special education classes are afforded professional evaluation before placement. Since it is the parents who often know the child better and care more about his or her welfare than anyone else, they too should have a say.

Judicially imposed procedural due process safeguards are not the best mechanism for insuring professional evaluation and parental input. While parents often are given a right to participate in the proceeding and to be professionally represented, they may not be able to communicate in a formal setting or may not be able to afford the price of a professional evaluator to represent them. Furthermore, some parents may not invoke the due process procedures either because they simply want to be rid of the child or because they assume that the school's decision is "best" for the child. Finally, courts cannot continually supervise the child's development and are not in a position to arrange for monitoring and reevaluations at later dates.[18]

The experience of due process rights in the special education setting probably provides the closest analogy to what can be expected with the administration of social services under Title XX. Parents seeking special education services are in the same position as persons seeking social services. In both cases, the person is usually confronted by more than one bureaucracy because he or she needs services delivered by several agencies. In addition, special education and social services agencies share many characteristics. Both are highly decentralized, highly discretionary professional organizations engaged in expert evaluations and judgments about classifying symptoms and prescribing treatment programs. Organizations such as these operate under vague guidelines and are not readily suscepti-

---

[18]Kirp *et al.* conclude that rather than impose judicialized due process rights, other states should adopt the California system. Although the study showed that some California officials do not follow their own procedures and although decisions are often made informally, a quality-control system of monitoring the actions of local officials could be instituted. Such a system, which would insure that genuine parental consent is obtained and that annual professional reevaluation is undertaken, would best provide for professional and parental input and would likely result in more accurate decisions regarding placement in special education. On the other hand, such a system requires the expenditure of greater resources than most states now commit to special education, and hence it is unlikely that widespread adoption of such a system will occur in the near future.

ble to monitoring, evaluation, or control. As discussed in Chapter 1, organizations of this type are characterized by competition among individuals and groups within the organization, each pushing for pet goals; the system functions by informal bargaining and adjustments, rather than by adherence to rules.

Furthermore, both types of agencies provide continuing services. In special education, there is the on-going program and the need for continued evaluation of the child. Thus, when a parent obtains a favorable decision it is not necessarily a one-time proposition; there is a continuing relationship that affects the ability of the parent to challenge interim agency decisions while the child is still in the program. The school authorities can impose a whole range of informal sanctions, even without the knowledge of the parent. Under Title XX, too, there are often long-term relationships that raise problems similar to those in special education.

The vindication of rights in special education represents a command issued from an outside agency (in this case, the courts). As the Kirp study points out, not unexpectedly, the officials in the system (the teachers, administrators, and other professionals) are hostile and resentful toward this approach, and they have developed a variety of informal threats and sanctions to discourage the exercise of rights. On the other hand, in order to mount a challenge, the parents have to muster a considerable amount of legal and professional expertise to refute the position of the special education bureaucracy. Even if the parents prevail, the court is limited in what it can do. It will try to avoid making the substantive decision, and there are means whereby the agency can mitigate the effects of an adverse court ruling. Court orders are no different from legislative and administrative rules; they are commands to lower-level officials to behave in certain ways. In highly discretionary, professional organizations, rules have very limited effects. This applies to court orders as well.

The problems of challenging agency decisions and enforcing rules is applicable to social services agencies to the extent that the relationship is discretionary, professional, and continuing. Social services clients, however, face additional hurdles. Although exceptional children are present in all social classes, many parents who are challenging special education authorities are middle- or upper-middle class and highly motivated; they are battling to improve the life chances of their children. These parents are thus in a more favorable position to mobilize the resources necessary for an adversary challenge than is the average social service client. Even though Title XX social services extend to the middle class, a great many, if not most, social services clients will be either poor or fairly close to the poverty line. Motivations and objectives may also be less clear-cut. For example, for a variety of reasons usually related to past failures, many of the poor have fears and ambivalent feelings concerning job training and employment, and they lack confidence in their ability to succeed. If told by officials that they cannot succeed, they may be less willing to fight that decision than is the parent of an exceptional child who is denied special education.

Studies of the exercise of due process rights in other contexts generally lead to the same conclusions found in the welfare and special education studies. The general finding is that when an individual confronts an institutional litigant in an adversary situation, the individual is at a disadvantage despite the formal procedural equality provided by the legal system (Galanter, 1974). The disparity between the parties varies with the circumstances. Clients are most disadvantaged when they not only confront an institutional litigant but are themselves residents of the institution. Thus, hospital and mental health patients, prisoners, and nursing home residents are, relatively speaking, worse off than are welfare recipients and social services clients, who, in turn, are worse off than Social Security applicants. In general, it is very difficult for a client to exercise his legal rights when he is faced with institutional adversaries who exercise discretionary authority over the things that he needs and wants. For the institutionalized client who is fighting the institution, such a challenge is almost impossible (see *Yale Law Journal,* 1975; Zander, 1976).

SUMMARY AND CONCLUSIONS

The fair hearing system is most successful in protecting individual rights when clients have the requisite information and resources, especially skilled counsel. The client is also likely to be most successful when his problem is a short-term one that does not require continuous monitoring or repeated discretionary decisions. Fair hearings are also more likely to succeed where eligibility is fairly clear-cut and where decisions do not involve great amounts of professional expertise. In sum, there are many situations in which the fair hearing system is an effective remedy for clients if the client possesses sufficient information and resources. In addition, even in those situations less favorable to fair hearings, the client's willingness to use the remedy increases his bargaining leverage. Certainly in close cases agencies will carefully consider conceding to client demands rather than incur the costs of litigating and possibly losing. Unfortunately, concessions from the agency do not have precedential effects, and the agencies can usually count on the ignorance of other recipients. The fair hearing system allows the agency to respond to those complaining clients, who are most able to help themselves, at the cost of shifting resources from those who may be in greater need of help.

Perhaps the most debilitating influence on the use of fair hearings as a remedy is the sheer number of hearings held. As the New York City study shows, backlogs, long waiting times, and delays in processing cases serve to set up barriers to the use of hearings. People will reckon into the costs of pursuing their rights the unpleasantness of the hearing experience itself. And assuming that clients can muster the resources to prosecute one appeal, how many clients can pursue the matter through a second appeal if the first decision is adverse, and then pursue a judicial remedy too?

Fair hearings would also seem to be a doubtful remedy when used to challenge decisions that involve professional discretion or expertise. For example, decisions about whether or not to provide special education, job training, various kinds of counseling, day care, and the like are very difficult to challenge in a fair hearing, since judgments of this type are so discretionary and are difficult to refute to the satisfaction of a disinterested hearing examiner. In those service areas that depend on the expertise of non-social-work professionals, such as special education and mental health, successful challenges can be mounted, but only if the complaining client is able to muster his own experts. This is likely to occur only if the matter is brought by an organization as a test case.

The study of procedural rights in special education in California pointed out another serious impediment to reliance upon hearings: the use of threats to chill the exercise of rights and the informal settlement of disputes. The scope of the jurisdiction of Title XX agencies gives them access to an enormous range of benefits and sanctions that can be used to bargain people out of their rights. Often, the mere threat of withholding a particular service or of forcing a client to accept an unwanted service is enough to make the client drop his demand. In addition, the overwhelming majority of disputes are settled informally rather than through formal hearing procedures. Such informality gives the agency even more leverage than the formal fair hearing system because the informal system is closed and off the record. There is no disinterested hearing examiner present to protect the client's interests, and there are no witnesses to be confronted and cross-examined. The client is thus placed in a dilemma. He must balance possible gains from being cooperative and friendly with the official, who insists that the two of them can adjust their differences, against the possible losses he may incur if he pursues his procedural rights.

As ineffective as fair hearings presently are, they may be further restricted in the future. Given the attitudes of the present Supreme Court, it
seems entirely possible to restrict fair hearings without violating the Due
Process Clause. Two approaches could be taken. One would be to change
the legal character of social services benefits so that they are no longer
considered property; they would be treated in the same manner as contracts at will in the *Bishop* case. The other approach would be to say that
even if social services are property interests, their nature is such that only
minimal due process procedures are required to safeguard them. The
present HEW regulations on fair hearings purport to codify the *Goldberg*
case, but *Goldberg* applied only to a "brutal need" situation. If the interest
of the recipient is perceived to be less important, then fewer due process
safeguards are needed. The Supreme Court has taken this approach in
several cases. In *Mathews* v. *Eldridge,* for example, the Court refused to
apply the *Goldberg* brutal-need test to the termination of disability benefits; the Court has also refused to apply *Goldberg* to the loss of a job.

Where, then, do the various social services fit? The denial of some social
services can have an immediate, severe impact; for example, the denial of
a mental health placement could result in institutionalization of a child. But
many social services probably would not have so immediate and irreparable an effect. In two cases, the Supreme Court was willing to leave the
claimants to whatever general relief they could find despite the fact that in
both situations there was considerable hardship. It is doubtful whether the
present Supreme Court would view denials of day care, homemaker services, counseling, family planning, job training, meals-on-wheels, or a large
variety of other social services as more important than loss of disability pay
or loss of a job.

If such an approach were to be taken, fair hearing regulations could be
cut back sharply for a great many social services. Clearly, pretermination
hearings could be eliminated, following *Mathews* v. *Eldridge.* This alone
would be a serious blow to the protection of client rights. It is also possible
that the right to oral presentation could be greatly reduced, especially for
decisions that require professional expertise, and that disinterested hearing
examiners and written records could be dispensed with.

In view of the changed attitude on the part of the Supreme Court, the
fact that the states want power to set up their own fair hearing systems, or
at least have a different federal system for Title XX is disturbing. Thus far,
however, HEW has resisted state pressure. For example, in its recently
proposed regulations dealing with fair hearings, HEW still insists on uniform hearing requirements with a fair amount of procedural protection. On

the other hand, discretion is granted to the states to discontinue a Title XX service pending the outcome of the hearing unless such a discontinuance would "impair the recipient's ability to continue an independent living arrangement or maintain employment [Federal Register, 1976]."[19] Whether HEW will ultimately prevail on the fair hearing controversy is unclear. Over the decades, the states have been able to prevail over HEW in most important conflicts over welfare policy. Prior to the recent Supreme Court decisions, HEW could argue that its fair hearing regulations were mandated by Goldberg, but this argument is no longer valid. The contest over the shape and content of fair hearings will now have to rely on the political process instead of the courts.

At the present time, there exists a fair hearing system for Title XX which on its face provides a considerable amount of client protection but in practice is weak and ineffectual. But even this system is now in danger of being sharply reduced, if not scuttled. The system is opposed by the states and has lost the support of the courts. At the present time, clients have great difficulty in protecting themselves from discretionary government decisions; in the future, these difficulties may even increase.

Clearly one line of defense may be to preserve what is already on the books, even though it is a weak form of protection. This would be a short-run strategy if pressure mounts to cut back on fair hearing procedures. The following chapters are concerned with how client protection can be strengthened by improving the fair hearing system and by devising other protective mechanisms. We shall also explore other systems of controlling official discretion in Title XX. Protecting client interests in social services is only one aspect of the more general problem of enforcing lower-level compliance with rules and standards.

---

[19]This proposed regulation has been withdrawn and, at this time, it is unclear what HEW will do.

II

Legal and Structural Remedies

4

Advocacy Resources and Other Client Assistance Programs

This chapter, as well as Chapters 5 and 6, deals with the use of various mechanisms and strategies to control discretion in social services. Fair hearings, imperfect as they are in operation, remain critical to the protection of the rights of individual clients. It is for this reason that I first discuss reforms in the hearing system itself and then go on to consider other proposals for changing or modifying the social service delivery system.

As I noted in Chapter 3, one of the most severe impediments to the fair hearing system is the clients' relative lack of resources, vis-à-vis the bureaucracy, either to pursue a remedy or to protect themselves from retaliation. The first section of this chapter deals with legal resources available to correct this imbalance between the client and the bureaucracy.

ADVOCACY RESOURCES

The Legal Profession

It is probably not an exaggeration to claim that OEO Legal Services lawyers resurrected the fair hearing system, and whatever promise that system has is due to the efforts of poverty lawyers (Gellhorn, 1967). When these lawyers were available to use the system, by and large they used it well and to the good advantage of their clients. To the extent that these lawyers have been available and willing to take social services cases, client resource problems have been greatly lessened.

The Legal Services Program, begun in 1965 during the War on Poverty years, represented a sharp break in many respects from traditional legal aid for the poor. The moving forces in Legal Services had an orientation and perspective different from that of traditional legal aid. One of the strongest ideological influences on OEO Legal Services was Mobilization for Youth, a social services community group located in New York City, which had a legal unit specializing in the problems of welfare recipients. Following this example, Legal Services offices not only took welfare cases but were instrumental in the adoption by growing welfare rights organizations of the concepts of the new property discussed in Chapter 1 and of fair hearings as a basic organizing tool.

Legal Services grew rapidly between 1965 and 1972, employing about 2000 lawyers. Thereafter, because of political difficulties, its funding remained fixed until 1976, when the program was reorganized under the Legal Services Corporation Act and funding was increased to $88 million per year.[1] During the years when Legal Services was in disarray at the national level, the field offices, by and large, remained active and reasonably healthy. With the reorganization and fresh leadership under the corporation at the national level, the outlook for Legal Services is promising. Funding is likely at least to remain at its present level and perhaps even to increase somewhat. The discussion that follows assumes that the present size and activity of Legal Services is a realistic estimate of what aid to social services clients will be available from this source.

How important a resource is Legal Services? The program currently employs about 3000 lawyers, and probably half as many paraprofessionals or legal workers, law students, and volunteer lawyers. The program handles about 1,300,000 cases per year (Klaus, 1976, p. 132). However, Legal Services lawyers handle matters other than welfare; in fact, most of their time is devoted to family law, consumer issues, and housing. The lawyers themselves report that less than 15% of their time is spent on welfare cases, and that these are mostly AFDC cases rather than social services cases (see Handler *et al.*, 1978, chap. 3). But perhaps the most serious limitation on

---

[1]For a discussion of the origins and development of OEO Legal Services, see Handler *et al.* (1978).

Legal Services, as a Title XX resource, is its case load. The programs are seriously overburdened. Estimates of legal needs in society are difficult to make, but a commonly cited statistic is that Legal Services, at its present level, meets only about one-fifth of the need of poor people (Klaus, 1976, p. 137). Furthermore, Legal Services programs are not evenly distributed throughout the country. There are many areas, especially in the South, with large concentrations of the poor, where there are few or no programs at all. Currently, there are about 17 metropolitan areas in the United States with populations in excess of 100,000 that have no Legal Services program. According to William Klaus (1976), an estimated 25 million people were eligible for Legal Services in 1971, and with the recession, this figure undoubtedly went higher. Even so, if 20% of those eligible received professional services at an average cost of $100 per case, the funding for the Legal Services Corporation would have to be increased to $500 million. Even if these estimates are inflated, they do indicate that Title XX cases will have a difficult time competing for scarce resources.

In addition to handling other problems of the poor, Legal Services lawyers have to weigh the importance of social services claims against income maintenance claims. The press of business tends to force lawyers to take familiar problems, which can be disposed of more efficiently, rather than to take new problems under Title XX. In sum, although Legal Services has been and continues to be of vital help to the poor, it is doubtful under present circumstances whether a great deal of aid from this source will be available for Title XX clients.

Title XX funds can be used for Legal Services because HEW regulations provide that funds can be made available for "providing advocacy, including legal services, to assure receipt of rights and entitlement due to adults at risk [Federal Register, 1975]." Thus far, grants have been made to over 50 projects. The total amount is somewhat in excess of $11 million, which is equal to over 10% of the Legal Services Corporation annual budget. Clearly, Title XX money is beginning to figure prominently in providing legal services.

The use of this money, however, raises a number of questions. When Title XX money became available, several Legal Services projects were able to obtain grants because of their ability to mobilize grant proposals more quickly than other social services agencies. But in the future, as other agencies become better organized, Legal Services will find itself surrounded by more competition, and there is no guarantee that present funding levels will increase or even continue. There is also the problem of strings attached to the Title XX money. For most of its existence, Legal

Services has had to wage a vigorous battle to preserve its independence from various branches of government; the program was threatened by Congresswoman Green, Vice President Agnew, and Governor Reagan, and it was close to death during the Nixon administration. The present uneasy solution is an independent government corporation. Title XX money may very well rekindle the old battles.

Recently, Georgia withdrew $1 million of Title XX money from the state-wide Legal Services program allegedly because of the aggressive representation of consumers and Medicaid recipients. In another program, Title XX money cannot be used for class actions. In other states, there have been shifts of money previously given to Legal Services. State Title XX agencies have wide discretion as to what state projects will be funded, so the independence of Legal Services projects will vary with the political leadership in the state. (Other constraints on the use of Title XX money are discussed in Chapter 5.)

In addition to Legal Services, there is the Judicare program, under which private attorneys take cases for the poor and are paid by the government according to fixed schedules. Although Judicare schedules cover Title XX cases, there are presently very few Judicare programs—none in large urban areas—and, as with Legal Services, eligibility ceilings are very low.[2]

There are also associations of private lawyers, sponsored by the organized bar, which provide legal services for the poor. These organizations are large, many lawyers participate, and a number of clients are served; however, there are only a few such programs in existence, and they are located only in three or four major cities (see Handler et al., 1978, chap. 3).

Another problem is that, unlike some other Title XX services, Legal Services are unavailable to middle-income persons because of low eligibility criteria. Thus, there is the problem of the private bar's willingness to serve Title XX clients who are above the poverty line. Many commentators have noted that it is most difficult for the families with moderate means to obtain adequate legal services, largely because the private bar predominantly serves the wealthy (see Frank, 1976). There are a number of developments which could result in the extension of professional services to people of moderate means. However, it is unclear whether any of these would also include Title XX cases.

One response to this squeezing out of middle-income people has been the emergence of a variety of prepaid and group plans which offer profes-

[2]For a description of the Judicare program, see Bractel (1974).

sional services to members at rates lower than those charged by lawyers in private practice. It is estimated that in 1975 there were over one million people covered under the 75 best-known plans. Of these plans, 29 were composed of union members, 9 of teachers, 13 of consumers, and 21 of students. In addition, efforts to standardize practice, specialization, and the use of paralegals could serve to reduce the cost of lawyers. Finally, there has been an enormous growth in the number of recent law school graduates and of students attending law schools. These people will be looking for work, and with the recent liberalization of the bans on advertising, perhaps legal fees will come down (Frank, 1976). But whether any of these developments will inure to Title XX recipients is unclear. Again, it is a question of priorities.

Private lawyers also engage in what is called pro bono work, or legal work for a reduced fee or for no fee.[3] It is the private bar's professional charitable contribution. Based on the lawyers' self-reporting, it is estimated that the bar spends about 6% of its working day on pro bono work. Most of this work is office counseling for individuals on family and other civil matters. Such pro bono work could cover Title XX cases, especially if the client's problems could be solved through negotiation. Typically, the pro bono work of lawyers does not involve litigation either before courts or administrative agencies, and therefore would exclude fair hearing representation.

In sum, looking at the legal profession—both Legal Services and the private bar—there may be resources sufficient to handle Title XX cases, but at the present time they are not mobilized to meet the need. Lawyers can do this work, and do it well, as the fair hearing experience with welfare shows. The question is whether similar services can be provided by other, less costly means. At the present time, lawyers are overtrained for many of the cases they handle; such cases could be handled as efficiently and at lower cost by people with less training. This leads us to consider the next potential resource for Title XX clients—the use of paraprofessionals.

Paralegals and Lay Advocates

This group includes a wide variety of people who have various amounts of training and who perform a range of law-related tasks. It covers legal secretaries who are skilled in processing all kinds of legal documents, as well as people with college or graduate degrees in paralegal training. Be-

---

[3]For a description of the private bar's pro bono work, see Handler et al. (1978, chap. 5).

cause of the variability in definition, training, and tasks, it is difficult to come up with precise figures on the number of paralegals in the country; but the number is not inconsiderable. According to U.S. Civil Service Commission estimates, there are 30,000 nonlawyers working in law-related jobs in the federal government. Legal Services employs about 1500 paralegals. There are over 50 formal paralegal training programs in the country and one, in Philadelphia, has already graduated 1000 students, most of whom are placed in private practice (Frank, 1976, pp. 117–118).

Lester Brickman (1971) has listed and described a variety of paralegal or lay advocate organizations. In welfare services, it was recognized early that because of economic considerations, nonlawyers had to be trained to help welfare recipients. Brickman reports "several score if not . . . hundreds" of training programs for lay advocates to represent welfare recipients. Many law-school clinical programs provide student representation in welfare cases, and there are various programs connected with community centers and neighborhood groups. In the consumer area, there are lay advocate groups that engage in a great deal of preventive law, debt counseling, conflict resolution between consumers and merchants, and the organization of consumer groups. In addition, use of paraprofessional specialists by government agencies that have consumer protection functions has grown. The Federal Trade Commission, for example, now has consumer protection specialists to assist the field offices in investigating violations of law and in responding to consumer complaints. City and state governments have also trained consumer protection specialists to carry out law-related work, and consumer specialists have also been part of OEO Legal Services. Brickman reports on one well-thought-out plan developed for the New Haven Legal Aid Bureau. The Debt and Credit Manager, a nonlawyer, assists debtor clients in managing their debts, keeping up with payments, and going through bankruptcy.

In the health area, the Bronx (New York) Community Health Advocacy Department (CHAD) provides health advocacy services as part of a health care center. In addition to performing advocacy work to obtain health services for the client, the health advocate sensitizes other members of the health team to issues of client dignity and privacy. The advocate is also useful in obtaining related, nonhealth services. For example, Brickman reports that when the health specialist determines that an elderly person needs a ground-level apartment, the lay advocate will try to find such an apartment. If public housing is available, the lay advocate will try to get a unit serviced by an elevator. CHAD has also organized and conducted educational campaigns to teach people about their rights concerning health issues, and has started a health advocacy program in a local hospital.

The California Rural Legal Assistance Senior Citizens' Project, an OEO program, also developed a health advocacy program for the elderly. The health advocate, after learning the applicable rules and regulations of the relevant agencies and services, represents the elderly before agencies, helps them apply for services, and helps prepare cases that are considered complex enough to require the attention of a lawyer.

The National Council of Senior Citizens funds legal services which include lay advocacy for a variety of purposes not restricted to health issues. There are also lay advocacy programs that deal with juvenile delinquency and related youth problems, prisoner rehabilitation, and probation and parole. Although at the time that Brickman wrote he found no lay advocacy projects specializing in housing, many of the current projects train lay advocates in housing matters.

Lay advocate programs vary from permanent, well-structured, and well-financed projects to ad hoc groups formed to meet a particular crisis. One noteworthy example of the latter was the Queens (New York) Lay Advocate Service which arose in response to the New York City school decentralization controversy. During one particular period, there were numerous suspensions of students; the group was formed by volunteers to accompany parents and students to the hearings, to help them examine records, and to work on correcting student placements. Law students prepared a manual to assist the lay advocates, and some lawyers held training sessions for them (Brickman, 1971, p. 1189).

In some programs lay advocates or paralegals work very closely with lawyers who supervise all of the work; in other programs, however, contact with lawyers is sporadic, and the lay advocate engages in what is essentially lawyering work. Such use of lay advocates raises the problem of the unauthorized practice of law. As a result of such concerns, the American Bar Association has established an accreditation program that could serve to discourage the development of paralegal or lay advocate training programs (Frank, 1976, p. 121).

The usefulness of lay advocates for Title XX cases seems beyond question. It has been shown that lay advocates can be trained to operate effectively in a variety of administrative situations which approximate social services cases. There are many tasks which are purely informational and which require trained community workers to make people aware of the availability of social services and of the laws and regulations governing the various programs. Trained people are needed to accompany clients to agencies, negotiation conferences, and hearings. Finally, there is need for specialists who know when the services of a lawyer are required, where to go to find one, and how to prepare the case for the lawyers. In all of these tasks, lay advocates in welfare, consumer matters, health, and housing have functioned well. They have performed services when lawyers were not available, or where the problems did not require the expertise of a lawyer.

To a great extent, the success of lay advocates depends on simplification of the legal system. To the extent that legal problems can be routinized or simplified, they can be handled more efficiently by nonlawyer specialists. This has been shown to be the case with automobile accidents, probate, divorce, and real estate transactions, and other legal problems. In Chapter 6, which deals with structural problems, the issue of simplifying the laws and regulations relating to social services is discussed. One of the benefits of such a simplification would be to aid client protection by making better use of lay advocates.

Self-Help

Another aspect of lay advocacy is the development of educational programs in various communities. OEO lawyers, at an early date, were successful in training welfare recipients to teach other recipients about their rights and to assist them in fair hearings. A necessary by-product of this endeavor was that the recipients themselves learned about their rights and how to take care of themselves. Community legal education programs have been conducted from time to time in areas such as consumer, juvenile and student rights, and housing. Although it is difficult to make estimates as to the number of these often unstructured, informal, and temporary efforts, the basic idea is sound since much of the law relating to client benefits and services can be simplified and made understandable to the uneducated lay person. People can be made aware of their rights and of the laws and regulations governing the agencies they deal with.

Democratizing legal knowledge is important for a number of reasons. Even if more funds become available for Legal Services and for other kinds of professional and paraprofessional resources, there still will not be enough of these resources for the poor and near-poor. Furthermore, for the reasons already discussed, social services clients will not or cannot turn to outside resources. Many conflicts are settled at the informal, negotiating stage, at which it would be inappropriate or unwise to raise the level of conflict by bringing in outside help. The client may feel that he will be better off handling the matter on his own. But in order to do that well, he should have knowledge and understanding of his rights and of the laws and regulations governing the behavior of the official and the agency. If the client knows and discloses agency rules which support his position, he will be in a far better bargaining situation than without this knowledge.

Another reason for self-help is that the applicable agency procedures in a given case may not provide for outside counsel. Given the Supreme Court's retreat from the formal hearing requirements of *Goldberg* v. *Kelly,* it may be that for many types of social services decisions only informal "give-and-take" hearings will be provided, at least at the initial administrative level, which, for most social services clients, is the only place where an appeal will be heard. Counsel, and perhaps even lay advocates, may not be allowed at these initial hearings. Needless to say, if a system of informal fair hearings without counsel or other professional assistance develops, social services clients will be at a great disadvantage. The agency, even though also represented by nonlawyers, will have experienced, skilled advocates. This is another important reason why social services clients themselves have to become aware of their legal rights and of the applicable laws and regulations.

Conclusions

There are a number of routes that HEW and the state Title XX agencies can take to improve client resources and to enhance client protection. There is authority in Title XX to provide legal services, but the threshold question is whether Title XX agencies should do so. It is anomalous for a government program to fund lawyers who are going to challenge that same government agency. During the early and tumultous days of the War on Poverty, when several Community Action Programs (CAP) were attacking local governments, the cry of conflict of interest was raised and great political pressure was put on CAP agencies to cease such activities. In recent years, however, there has developed greater sophistication about the role of legal rights and client protection before government agencies. Specifically, the rise of public interest law has had an important influence on the provision of legal services.

Public interest law is a varied and interesting phenomenon with diverse strands and roots. The part that is relevant here stresses the importance of providing legal services for traditionally underrepresented groups in American society. Most prominent and noteworthy among the public interest law cases have been those dealing with consumer and environmental issues, but public interest law has also represented the poor, minorities, the handicapped, and women. It is now accepted dogma that the public interest is best served if underrepresented groups are represented before government agencies. A few important federal regulatory agencies, such as the Interstate Commerce Commission and the Federal Communications Commission, have established programs whereby counsel is now provided at government expense to help individuals present their grievances to the agencies. Other agencies, such as the Nuclear Regulatory Commission, are considering allocating funds to pay the legal fees of groups that bring lawsuits against them. There is ample precedent, then, both in theory and in practice, for Title XX agencies to fund legal resources for clients to vindicate their legal rights before the agencies.[4]

There are a number of ways in which Title XX funds could be used to strengthen the capacity of Legal Services to handle social services cases. As stated earlier, there are heavy demands on Legal Services offices, and there is a question as to what priority social services cases would have as compared to income maintenance issues, health care, employment, or housing. Therefore, any Title XX money should be specifically earmarked for social services cases. Depending on their type, Legal Services organizations have a unique capacity in three areas.

First, they have done excellent law reform work (i.e., class actions or test cases) on behalf of the poor, and there are many Title XX questions of general applicability that will need to be tested. Test case litigation, when done by the private bar, is extremely costly, and private lawyers usually are not available to handle the main responsibilities of these cases as part of their pro bono work. Several Legal Services offices are equipped to handle such cases, and at a much lower cost.

A second area in which Legal Services excels is in the traditional service (i.e., a one-time case, such as a divorce, for an individual client); such cases, of course, are the staples of Legal Services business. Many of the offices have created procedures which allow them to handle large numbers of service cases on an efficient basis. Title XX agencies can purchase some of the service work of Legal Services, an arrangement which would be particularly beneficial to both Legal Services and Title XX. The new Legal Services Corporation is looking for alternative funding sources, and Title XX can tap an already existing pool of service-case-oriented lawyers.

---

[4]For a discussion of public interest law, see Handler et al. (1978, chap. 4) and Weisbrod et al. (1978).

The third area in which several Legal Services programs have proved to be effective is in the training of lay advocates, community workers, and recipient populations. From time to time, Legal Services programs have conducted excellent training programs, prepared and distributed manuals, and conducted informational and educational programs. All of these skills can be used in Title XX work.

As noted earlier, however, Legal Services are not evenly spread throughout the country. Furthermore, there is great variation in the quality and capacity of the various offices. All offices have a service capacity, but far fewer can handle law reform and lay advocacy training. Therefore, Title XX agencies must look to other legal resources for their clients.

Where Judicare programs exist, funds can be provided to pay private lawyers for Title XX cases. These lawyers cannot be expected to engage in test case litigation or much lay advocacy training; the Judicare program, by and large, is not set up or financed for that kind of work. But in certain parts of the country, particularly in outlying areas, Judicare lawyers can provide legal help for the poor on social services cases.

The private bar can also be utilized in a number of ways. In some of the major metropolitan areas, there are extensive programs in which volunteer lawyers engage in referral work or in the direct provision of legal services. These organizations present a private alternative to publicly supported legal services for the poor, and they should be utilized by Title XX agencies. Thus social services can be tied into the referral network, probably at slight additional cost, and service work can be purchased.

The private bar can also be used for test case litigation if Title XX agencies are willing to pay for it. This can be done in two different ways. There are law reform organizations that can do Title XX law reform work on a project basis; thus, Title XX agencies could approach the ACLU, the NAACP, or the Lawyers Committee for Civil Rights Under Law, to name some of the more prominent organizations. In addition, Title XX agencies can make provision to pay attorneys' fees for public-interest-law cases that are related to Title XX. As noted earlier, some employment discrimination, civil rights, and environmental statutes already provide for the payment of attorneys' fees under certain specified conditions which, generally speaking, restrict fees to important cases where the plaintiff prevails. Such statutes are not general invitations to lawyers to make money, but are designed to encourage the useful testing of legal questions and the vindication of legal rights by people and groups that would otherwise lack the resources to do so. The same principles could apply to Title XX.

Law school clinical programs can also be used as a Title XX resource. Over the past several years, there has been an enormous increase in the funding of clinical programs in law schools. These programs concentrate on field-level service case work. Although the subject matter of student clinical work varies, the concentration is on the problems of the poor, including welfare, housing, and juvenile delinquency. These programs could be encouraged to handle more social services cases.

Title XX agencies can also seek out and support paralegal and lay advocacy programs. The agencies can purchase the services of programs already underway, or they can facilitate new programs in areas where legal resources are in short supply. Again, there is no lack of technical experience for paralegal and lay advocacy programs; the problem is the lack of will to embark on such endeavors and the lack of funding. Because many social service problems do not require a lawyer and are probably better handled by lay persons, Title XX support of these programs should expand significantly. In those areas of the country where strong lawyer resources, such as Legal Services programs, already exist, perhaps the emphasis should be on paralegals who have some lawyer supervision. Where Legal Services are not available, or where the offices lack the capacity to supervise paralegals, more attention should be given to the free-standing, community-based model. Members of the private bar could be enlisted, either as volunteers or on salary, to lend assistance, supervision, and back-up services to the lay advocate organization.

Democratizing legal knowledge also can take a variety of forms. The citizen information center is an old and proven idea. It should be expanded to include legal rights in social services. In addition, Title XX agencies should support the development and teaching of legal rights related to social services in a variety of structural settings, as in schools of social work, secondary schools, adult education centers, recreation centers, clinics, and community houses.

In sum, there are many methods by which Title XX agencies can use their authority and funds to improve client resources for the protection of client rights. The essential point is that each agency should carefully assess not only the needs of its clients but also the available legal and paralegal resources in the various communities. Funding a Legal Services program for law reform will not work if the local Legal Services office lacks a law reform capacity; in such a situation, it is better to pay counsel fees to the prevailing party under certain specified conditions. Similarly, if the local private bar is organized to provide strong voluntary efforts, then the Title XX agency should explore the possibilities of building on the strength of that organization rather than working through an overburdened, low-quality Legal Services office.

ALTERNATIVES TO ADVERSARY REPRESENTATION

Ineffective use of the fair hearing system is partly the result of clients' lack of knowledge and legal resources. The other part of the problem is that clients find themselves in situations where the exercise of rights is chilled because of the structural set-up; they are in a continuing relationship with agency officials and fear retaliation. In such situations, making legal resources available will not suffice because the risks of using outside resources are perceived as too high by the clients. To remedy this kind of impediment to the exercise of legal rights, various internal governmental controls have been developed. Control units monitor and supervise the performance of the agencies and their lower-level officials and see that client interests are protected. Sometimes these controls are independent of a given department or agency; an example is the ombudsman. Others are part of an agency's own internal inspection unit or specifically designated advocacy unit. A control unit can be created to investigate specific instances of alleged malfeasance or can be a permanent part of government.

Wisconsin State District Director System

A useful way to illustrate how such a system works is to look at the role of the Wisconsin State District Director System, which existed prior to 1968 (see Handler, 1969). The Wisconsin AFDC program is administered by the counties. The state Department of Health and Social Services divided the state into 10 districts, each having a district director in charge of program development, liaison between the county agencies and the state agency, and general troubleshooting. District directors also played a key role in choosing personnel. For example, county government worked very closely with the district directors in selecting county welfare directors, and the district directors were also in charge of strengthening and maintaining the merit system for welfare department staff.

In addition to all of their other duties, the district directors had an important role in the fair hearing process. Whenever notice of a client complaint came to their attention, the directors would immediately interview the client and investigate the complaint. The state regulations referred to the district directors as "mediators" rather than "adjudicators" but, in fact, the directors worked hard at settling disputes between clients and the county agencies.

A statistical analysis of fair hearings in Wisconsin over a 25-year period showed that the district directors actively settled cases and that, generally speaking, clients prevailed more often when the directors were instrumental in reaching the settlement (Handler, 1969). Interviews with all of the directors revealed that they took pride in their fair hearing work and welcomed opportunities to help individual welfare clients.

There were also important structural reasons why the district directors were successful in their fair hearing work. Almost all of the directors had been promoted from the field—that is, they had spent varying amounts of time as caseworkers and as supervisors at the county agencies before they were hired by the state agency. Thus, when the directors came before the county agency in a fair hearing dispute, they came as experienced people and more importantly as officials who had other important supervisory duties with that agency. In other words, the district directors had discretionary authority and a continuing relationship with the county agency. Therefore, their analysis and recommendations carried weight with the county agencies.

In addition, district directors felt that benefits accrued to them from their fair hearing role, since client complaints were an additional method whereby they could uncover weaknesses in county administration. Most directors thought that clients were generally reluctant to file an appeal unless they had a fairly serious problem, so although there were occasional chronic malcontents, appeals usually did indicate a matter worth looking into. More often than not, the directors found that the counties were violating state agency regulations. Thus, the directors could both help clients and correct administrative misfeasance at the same time. In addition, at the time of the study, there were not many fair hearings; thus, the directors viewed the appeals as a change of pace and as an opportunity to talk to recipients. Even the older directors, who had been in their present positions for a long period of time, were not jaded by fair hearing appeals.

The result was that during the period studied, these state officials, the district directors, provided an important pro-client resource in disputes with county welfare agencies. The district directors were successful because, for the most part, they were sympathetic to client problems, they were knowledgeable and experienced, and they were powerful officials in their own right. Helping clients in the fair hearings also helped the directors to accomplish their other administrative tasks, namely, supervision of the county agencies. The question, then, is to what extent some or all of these structural conditions are necessary for internal, bureaucratic client advocates to function as successfully as did the Wisconsin state district directors. Would the directors have been as successful if client advocacy was their primary mission instead of being a minor part of their more important duties to oversee county agencies? Would the district directors have been as successful if the volume of fair hearing cases had been higher?

In 1969, the Wisconsin procedures became more formalized and the role of the district directors in fair hearings was eliminated. Following nationwide trends, the number of appeals filed increased, but client success rates dropped. Then, in 1974, the state introduced mediators in an effort to reduce the number of appeals filed (see Hammer and Hartley, 1978). Contrary to the expectations of the state, in those areas where mediators functioned, hearings increased, no-show rates dropped, and client success rates increased in both hearings and withdrawals. The effects of the mediators on helping clients was most pronounced in cases where disputes were over the sufficiency of the grant, or supplements or reductions, rather than termination or denial of entry.[5] The study concluded that the mediators supplied valuable information to the recipients, which greatly improved their chances of success. Since the mediators did not succeed in reducing the number of appeals, the program was eliminated by the state.

The Wisconsin state district director and mediator experiences illustrate the potentiality of an alternative mechanism for resolving conflicts between clients and bureaucracies. The principal difference between the district director system and the fair hearing system is that in the former the government supplies the resource for investigating the factual and legal matters of the dispute rather than rely on the aggrieved party to develop the claim. It is a form of investigative adjudication which has also been used in a variety of other contexts.

Ombudsmen

Although the first ombudsman was established in Sweden in 1809, the idea did not really spread until after 1955, when the first Danish om-

---

[5]It is not entirely clear why there was this difference. It may be that eligibility rules are more clear-cut. Since the recipient has the burden of persuading the hearing officer in the sufficiency, supplement, and reduction cases, it may also be that the information supplied by the mediators was a more valuable resource.

budsman began to proselytize on behalf of the institution; thereafter, variations of the Swedish and Danish models were established in over 21 countries.[6]

In both Sweden and Denmark, the ombudsman's function is to supervise the operations of government. Both ombudsmen receive and investigate citizen complaints or conduct investigations on their own. Both can also order the prosecution of officials who engage in serious misconduct; however, this power is rarely used. Although a large part of the work of the ombudsman consists of adjusting individual complaints and disputes, in both countries the ombudsman has been responsible for the implementation of more systemic institutional changes, such as standardization of procedures or modification of the organizational structure to make government operations more efficient and fair.

The ombudsmen in Sweden and Denmark rely principally on publicity. Their success depends on the prestige of their office, on a favorable press, and on the fact that officials are anxious to avoid unfavorable reports by the ombudsman. It is believed, especially in Sweden, that the ombudsman exerts an influence simply by virtue of the fact that he exists: People know that he is there to receive complaints and bureaucrats know that he can examine their records at any time without notice (see Gellhorn, 1966).

To what extent is the Swedish and Danish ombudsman system exportable? How has it fared in other countries and in other contexts? It is claimed that the ombudsman can function only in relatively small countries with homogeneous populations. Thus, it is argued, in a larger country such as Great Britain the ombudsman would be swamped with work and would be ineffective. Sweden solves this problem by having several ombudsmen with defined geographic and functional jurisdictions. Of course, the size of the ombudsman staff could also be increased.

But a more serious question about the viability of ombudsmen concerns the structural nature of the office. In Great Britain, for example, there are various criteria that must be met before the ombudsman will accept a case. Among these are that no adequate judicial remedy exists and that cases must be referred through a Member of Parliament. The purpose of this so-called M.P. filter is to weed out frivolous complaints, but some M.Ps. simply refer all complaints without screening them, and others have been known to use the ombudsman for political purposes. At any rate, the British ombudsman receives fewer complaints in absolute numbers than

---

[6]There are numerous descriptions of the ombudsmen. See Weisbrod *et al.* (1978, chap. 17), and Cappelletti (1975).

the Danish ombudsman despite a population 10 times larger. There could be many reasons for this relative disuse of the British system, among them lack of publicity and therefore of awareness on the part of the people, or less reason to complain. But it is also possible that Britons perceive the ombudsman as being too closely tied to the establishment because of the M.P. filter and intake restrictions (see Weisbrod et al., 1978).

There are many impressionistic accounts of the workings of the various ombudsman systems, but relatively few systematic, empirical studies. It is an institution with considerable variation and adaptability. To the extent that it is available to receive citizen complaints, investigate them, and act on them, it would seem, at least in theory, to provide a resource for complaining clients.

Perhaps the most significant ombudsman-type institution is the New Jersey Office of the Public Advocate, created in 1974. It is a cabinet-level department with six divisions: public defender; inmate advocacy and parole revocation; mental health advocacy; a rate counsel, who represents the public interest at utility hearings; public interest advocacy (i.e., law reform); and citizens' complaints and dispute settlement. This last division receives and investigates complaints from citizens concerning the action or inaction of any branch of government. A toll-free telephone number gives citizens easy access to the advocate's office. During its first 6 months of operation, the advocate's office received more than 3000 complaints. These fell into four categories: the ineffectiveness of a particular state agency, jurisdictional disputes between agencies, dissatisfaction with an agency decision, and lack of responsiveness by an agency. The New Jersey Public Advocate not only handles individual cases, but also has the authority to conduct investigations, to issue reports, and to lobby. It is too early to tell if the New Jersey experiment will succeed. A distinguished, experienced lawyer was appointed the first public advocate, and, not unexpectedly, his vigorous use of the office has made enemies in both the legislature and among his fellow cabinet officers (Trubek, 1976).

Another interesting experiment is the Wisconsin Lieutenant Governor's Nursing Home Ombudsman Project, which investigates and handles nursing home complaints and which studies broad problems of long-term care. Between 1972, the year of its inception, and 1975, the office investigated about 1900 different issues raised by about 3000 complainants. The largest proportion of claims were filed by relatives of patients and dealt with such complaints as neglect, abuse, violations of patient rights, poor staffing, and overcharging. The ombudsman reported that over one-half of the cases were resolved to the satisfaction of the complainants and less than

20% of the claims were invalid. In addition to handling individual complaints, the ombudsman engaged in a number of law reform efforts including proposed revision of state nursing home regulations, problems of chronic noncompliance, improvements in the licensing and certification inspection system, and exploring alternatives to long-term care. The office has also engaged in an extensive lobbying effort to improve state enforcement powers (Report of the Wisconsin Nursing Home Ombudsman Program, 1976).

Some hospitals have started using patient advocates as a result of interest in bills of rights for patients and increasing concern about patient dignity. However, hospital patient advocates are often employed by the hospitals and are restricted in the types of problems they can investigate. Patient advocates, for example, cannot inquire into doctor–patient relationships. Hospital patient advocates also probably suffer from the same disabilities as school social workers; that is, their dependence on the same institution that deals with the client qualifies their independence and vigor. If hospital patient advocates are dependent on the hospital administration for their jobs, then they may easily become tools used to "cool" patient complaints rather than remain true advocates.

Unlike many hospital patient advocacy programs where the advocate's position and independence are compromised because he is an employee of the hospital, the Wisconsin Nursing Home Ombudsman is an independent government agency not beholden to the nursing home industry. On the other hand, as is true of any regulatory agency, the nursing home ombudsman must have some political clout both within and without the state government or he will merely be ignored.

Another interesting ombudsman-type experiment has been tried in the courts. In 1971, as a result of public-interest-law litigation, the U.S. District Court in Alabama held that it is a violation of the Constitution to civilly commit people to mental institutions under the guise of providing treatment and then to fail to provide that treatment. By way of relief, the court ordered some 80 specific changes designed to improve the standard of treatment. These included increasing the staff, making physical improvements, designing and specifying treatment plans, and outlawing institutional peonage. The court's decision amounted to the establishment of a basic legal right to treatment and of a code of behavior to insure that the right would be implemented. It was obvious that in a mental institution one could not rely on complaining clients to implement their newly won charter, so the court established Human Rights Committees to monitor performance. The committees have been in existence for some time now with varying degrees of success. Not unexpectedly, a certain amount of hostility has developed between some of the committees and the institutions, but a 1975 study agrees that on the whole the committees have served a useful purpose in stimulating changes in hospital administration and treatment of patients (*Yale Law Journal,* 1975).

There has also been a significant development regarding ombudsmen in prisons. The Scandinavian ombudsmen, as part of their regular duties, hear and investigate complaints arising out of penal institutions. In the United States, some state-wide ombudsmen handle prison complaints, but there also are ombudsmen exclusively for prisons. The Oregon prison ombudsman is a regular staff member who is responsible to the prison superintendent; inmates must first use the normal grievance procedure and may petition the ombudsman only if the regular channels fail to respond in a reasonable time. In Philadelphia, the ombudsman project is run by the Pennsylvania Prison Society at the invitation of the Philadelphia Superintendent of Prisons. The ombudsman is an ex-inmate who receives and investigates complaints, conducts investigations on his own, and makes recommendations and periodic reports. Maryland has an Inmate Grievance Commission composed of five members appointed by the governor. As in the Oregon system, the inmate must first use the regular channels; only thereafter will the commission receive a complaint. The commission has the power to hold hearings and, with the approval of the Secretary of Public Safety, is given access to documentary evidence and the power to subpoena witnesses. The inmate can appear in person or with counsel (at his own expense) and can cross-examine witnesses. In addition to these ongoing projects, the Model Act for the Protection of Rights of Prisoners recommends that prisons maintain a person outside of the correction agency with the power to receive, investigate, and issue reports on complaints. There is also a California proposal for the creation of a Joint Legislative Committee on Correction Administration that would nominate an ombudsman to receive and investigate complaints (Tibbles, 1972).

HEW's Administration on Aging (AOA) has made grants to 48 projects for the development of ombudsman programs for nursing homes. In Wisconsin, Michigan, and five other states in which HEW had previously funded demonstration projects, the AOA nursing home ombudsman programs have enjoyed some success. In states without previous experience, the new programs have heavy responsibilities and slight resources. The programs must inform and coordinate local groups, monitor and shape legislation concerning nursing homes and the aged in general, and seek additional means of support. Some programs have undertaken to train large numbers of "nursing home visitors" who handle complaints in nursing homes; others have focused their attention on legislative reform; still others concentrate on regularizing their relations with the state departments on which they depend for access and enforcement under HEW rules. To date, most of these projects have been unable to focus on handling individual complaints. Ideally, the projects will lead to a network of coordinated local programs designed to handle individual complaints, with a central office in charge of legislative monitoring, state program supervision, and technical assistance support.

There are also ombudsman offices that are not tied to specific institutions but are available for use by the general public. In several cities (perhaps more than a dozen by now), there are what have come to be known as "little city halls," patterned after the Boston Mayor's Office of Public Services (Nordlinger, 1973; Wyner, 1973a; Moore, 1973). The Boston program comprises 14 offices located in all sections of the city, not just in the ghettoes; the average size of the community served is between 50 and 60,000 people. Originally, the offices were conceived of as being only complaint centers, but from the beginning citizens demonstrated a desire and need for various services. As a result, the offices presently act as information brokers, as referral agencies, and as advocacy agencies. Each office has a manager, an assistant, and two service coordinators. In addition, the fire department maintains a fire inspector in each office, there are housing department inspectors in many of the offices, and some federal agencies, such as the Social Security Administration, have part-time representatives. According to a 1970 study, over 20% of Boston households have used these little city halls, and there were over 160,000 "meaningful" contacts (defined as use of the office on more than one occasion). Poor families (i.e., those with incomes of less than $5000) use the offices less than those with higher incomes; the highest use was among families with incomes between $15,000 and $24,999. Still, one out of five families with incomes below $5000 did use the offices.

Chicago has established a Mayor's Office of Inquiry and Information staffed with 10 professionals plus clerical help. The office functions mainly as a broker, relaying citizen requests and complaints to appropriate agencies. Honolulu has an Office of Information and Complaint, which, in 1971, received over 900 inquiries per month. The office tries to mediate complaints, most of which involve municipal services such as street repairs, and garbage collection. There are also some state-wide offices, usually attached to the office of the lieutenant governor (Wyner, 1973b), which primarily handle complaints about welfare, employment, and licensing.

Oregon has established a state-wide executive ombudsman, appointed by the governor, whose duties include the investigation of complaints, the submission of recommendations to state agencies, the making of reports to the governor and the legislature, and the identification of patterns or clusters of problems. As of 1970, the highest proportion of complaints coming to the Oregon ombudsman involved welfare (Capps, 1973). There are also executive ombudsmen in Pennsylvania, Iowa, Puerto Rico, and Nassau County, New York (Mann, 1973; Liston, 1973; Burgess et al., 1973; Hannon, 1973).

Ombudsman proposals and projects are growing; clearly it is an idea with intriguing possibilities. Unfortunately, there have been few solid evaluative studies done on the performance of the various models. Some offices have been given good marks on statistical indicators of high use—number of contacts and referrals, number of repeat clients, and so forth—on the assumption that if the office were not performing some useful service for its clientele, they would not continue to use it. In other studies, specific examples are used to indicate an office's success; for example, the Iowa Social Services Department usually took 6 months or more to replace lost or stolen AFDC checks. The delay was a deliberate department policy used to check for fraud (that is, to wait to see if the original check was cashed) and to teach people not to lose their checks. This policy was investigated and publicized by the Iowa Citizens' Aide, and the department policy was changed to provide for reissuing of checks within 2 weeks (Liston, 1973, p. 180). On the other hand, some offices have been criticized for their lack of follow-up; they merely receive citizen complaints, pass them on, and do nothing else (Wyner, 1973a, p. 34). Some ombudsman offices have had problems because they lack any real power, and other offices are too closely tied to the local political structure to oppose officials in other parts of government (Mann, 1973, pp. 262–263; Wyner, 1973b, pp. 147–148; Hannon, 1973, pp. 125–126, 129–130).

In summary, the provision of informal administrative support for clients can take various forms. No one formula is suitable for all situations, and different models will have to be experimented with in different situations. Each model has its strengths and weaknesses. Theoretically, one would doubt the independence and vigor of in-house advocates. The outside critic, particularly one with access to the media, might carry much more influence with a particular agency. On the other hand, a great deal of advocacy is best conducted through quiet negotiation by knowledgeable insiders rather than through aggressive confrontation. It is clear that models cannot be borrowed wholesale and be expected to work without considerable adjustment to a specific environment. What is important, though, is that there are many models to choose from in devising ways of providing internal administrative resources for clients and that they could be applied to the delivery of social services under Title XX.

Mediation and Arbitration[7]

Another possible alternative to the adversarial fair hearing system is the use of mediation or arbitration. There are three possible models: (a) mediation, in which a third party intervenes in the dispute to increase communication between the disputants and to facilitate bargaining, but the mediator lacks the power to impose a solution; (b) arbitration, in which the third party does have the power to impose a solution, but the proceedings are informal and flexible; and (c) investigative adjudication, in which the adjudicator takes an active role in investigating the dispute. All three of these techniques have been used in other societies as well as in the United States. Investigative adjudication is used in the civil law countries, while mediation and arbitration are widely used in this country in commercial and labor disputes. The question is to what extent these forms can be used for Title XX cases.

Mediation experiments have been undertaken or proposed for neighborhood conflicts, for consumer cases, and for social benefit conflicts. I have already described the Wisconsin experiment with using mediators in welfare disputes. An example in the criminal law area is the Columbus (Ohio) Night Prosecutor Program in which the complainant and the accused, who are often family members or neighbors, are given an opportunity to try to settle their problems before the criminal process is started. The program provides mediation services and has been successful in resolving at least temporarily a great many incidents that normally give rise to criminal charges. The program also provides follow-up services which attempt to reach the underlying causes of the dispute. It has been suggested that there are many disputes in our society that could be handled through mediation, and there is a call for establishment of informal neighborhood courts to provide mediation resources. Such mediation would be voluntary; the parties would be encouraged to use the neighborhood courts, but would not be precluded from using more formal dispute-settling procedures.

---

[7]For a wide-ranging discussion of a variety of third-party techniques to resolve disputes see Jaffe (1978). Many of the examples in the text are based on this source.

The use of mediation is being experimented with in the area of consumer complaints. For the reasons discussed earlier, there is growing evidence that the small claims court has not worked out as planned; part of the problem, it is felt, is that it relies on the adversary system. In Sweden, there are experiments with Public Complaint Boards composed of consumer and merchant representatives. Consumer complaints are investigated by the staff, which then issues a statement on the merits of the complaint with or without a nonbinding recommendation as to how the matter should be settled. The system then relies on the parties to bargain, but there is available a simplified small-claims procedure. It is claimed that the results of the Swedish Public Complaint Boards are highly successful; over 80% of all claims are settled without resort to the formal procedure.

There seems to be no reason why mediation cannot be used to deal with Title XX disputes. Title XX agencies could experiment with free-standing mediation services, perhaps structured after the Swedish Public Complaint Boards. Mediation services would not supplant fair hearings under the Social Security Act, but many complaints might be satisfactorily settled through mediation without resort to the fair hearing system.

Arbitration can be successful because it provides a more expeditious settlement of disputes than the more cumbersome judicial procedure, and quite often the arbitrators are people who have had experience with the issues in dispute. On the basis of these qualities, it is possible to conclude that arbitration has few advantages over the fair hearing system, which is already a fairly simple system with hearing examiners who are specialists. Complexity, however, is a matter of degree; even though the fair hearing system is far less complex than a judicial trial, it still may be a forbidding, complex system from the point of view of the recipient. Thus, it may be that an arbitration system incorporated into a neighborhood court or a citizen's complaint board would be an improvement on the fair hearing system, especially in the large urban areas. There has been considerable interest in utilizing the experience of the American Arbitration Association in new areas and in combining arbitration with mediation services. The Association has been active in the handling of automobile accident cases and in election campaign disputes. Experiments have been launched to see how well arbitration functions in hospitals, in health maintenance organizations, and in family disputes. The National Center for Dispute Settlement, an offshoot of the American Arbitration Association, is attempting to apply techniques used in resolving labor–management conflicts to community problems, public employment, and a variety of civil matters. One of the premises of this organization is that lay people, trained in mediation techniques, can facilitate the handling of local problems.

The method of investigative adjudication is approximated by the Wisconsin District Director System, in which the directors took it upon themselves to investigate the allegations of the complaint. The value of this procedure is that the investigator has more resources than the complaining client and is better able to gather information. In many of the ombudsman experiments, ombudsmen perform investigative mediation–arbitration roles, and some scholars have called for application of investigative techniques to traditionally adversarial procedures, such as the processing of insurance claims (Whitford and Kimball, 1974). The New Jersey Public Advocate combines investigative functions with mediation; the same is true of the Swedish Public Complaint Board. Both offer mediation services, both investigate complaints, and both can also adjudicate disputes.

SUMMARY

This chapter discusses two different approaches to meeting some of the deficiencies of fair hearings. One approach assumes that the present fair hearing structure will continue to exist, but seeks to improve the resources available for the client. Among these resources are: (a) Legal Services attorneys who can be induced to undertake more Title XX cases; (b) attorneys in Judicare programs, in prepaid plans, and in private practice who might undertake Title XX work as part of their pro bono work; (c) paralegals and lay advocates, who can be trained to handle legal problems which do not require a lawyer; and (d) self-help programs.

The other approach looks to structural modification of the adversary system. Although the adversarial fair hearing system is the basic model, there are a variety of alternatives which are being used in a number of different contexts. Variations of the ombudsman are used to investigate all kinds of citizen complaints. Ombudsman projects can be general government investigators, such as the New Jersey Office of the Public Advocate, or they can deal with a specific area, such as nursing homes. Some ombudsman are formally constituted officers; others are informal and operate out of a mayor's office. Most are publicly financed, but there are also privately sponsored ombudsmen. The common characteristic, however, is that the aggrieved person is not solely responsible for working up his claim, as he is under the fair hearing system; rather, the ombudsman receives the complaint and then conducts the investigation.

Another kind of structural modification of the fair hearing system involves publicly or privately sponsored mediation and arbitration. Mediation and arbitration can be used in a variety of settings and can be effective supplementary dispute-settling mechanisms for clients who have complaints against social service agencies. There is no reason why the formal administrative hearing must be the exclusive system for adjudicating claims.

The discussion so far has explored ways of protecting client rights by limiting official discretion through the provision of resources to the client to enable him to challenge discretionary decisions. There are, however, other ways of limiting discretion, namely management and quality control, and structural alternatives for the delivery of social services. The next two chapters discuss these possibilities.

5

Management Supervision
and Quality Control:
Information, Efficiency,
and Privacy

Controlling bureaucratic discretion by strengthening client resources can be viewed as an attempt to reform the system from the bottom up. This chapter deals with attempts to control official discretion from the other end, from the vantage point of the policymakers and the upper-level managers.

There have been continuous efforts to improve quality control and to strengthen management supervision. The subject is vast and the details are beyond the scope of this book. However, it is of concern to the extent that it bears on the issue of client protection.

In theory, an argument can be made that in certain circumstances there is a coincidence of interests between management and the protection of client rights. One such situation is where lower-level decisions are covered by specific, clear rules; in many instances clients complain not about the wrongful exercise of discretion, but about the violation of clear rules such as antidiscrimination statutes. Assuming good faith on the part of upper-level management, their interest in legality coincides with the interests of those suffering from discrimination, and it makes little difference if discriminatory practices by lower-level officials are checked by supervisors or by a complaining client. In such situations, management's interest in ferreting out and correcting violations serves to vindicate client rights as well.

There are also many discretionary decisions that do not violate clear, specific rules. A great many rehabilitative social services decisions involve investigating complex factual matters and then applying factual conclusions to vague standards and policies. However, even when a decision is discretionary, clients still have the right to be treated fairly, the right to be heard, and other rights. Managers and controllers also have interests in how these decisions are made. Suppose, for example, that a particular agency is not sufficiently sensitive to the state's announced policy of encouraging employment training and it awards day care only to mothers who are employed full-time. Management would want to change these lower-level decisions to bring them more in line with state policy. It was noted in Chapter 4 that the Wisconsin State District Director System used client complaints as an additional method of uncovering and correcting county deviations from state policy. In these situations, to the extent that managers and controllers correct field-level decisions, client rights are also vindicated.

However, even though the efforts of managers and controllers can in some cases vindicate client rights, managers and controllers are not primarily concerned with individual cases; their primary concerns are how money is spent and how the program is carried out. Furthermore, as efficient administrators, they acknowledge and tolerate a certain amount of error. Their concern is with averages, not with individual justice. Despite this important difference in focus, management supervision and quality control are important for the protection of client rights insofar as these techniques are successful in reducing error. The problems of protecting client rights becomes more manageable when there are fewer violations resulting in fewer grievances and, therefore, less need for client protection. At least on a theoretical level, then, clients have an interest in both effective management and in the creation of quality control systems.

At the practical level, however, there are severe problems in devising and implementing effective management and quality control systems within the social service context, and these problems pose significant dangers to clients.[1] There are problems of devising accurate standards by which to measure the performance of an agency, and there are problems of gathering the information necessary to find out whether the standards are being met. The two sets of problems are interrelated but will be discussed separately.

---

[1]The literature on management and quality control techniques is vast, and a full treatment is beyond the scope of this work. For a critical analysis, see Self (1975).

DEFINING STANDARDS

The problem of defining standards is tied, of course, to the goals and purposes of the program. For example, if the purpose of day care is to enable parents to work, then the standard of performance for a particular decision allocating a day care slot is whether, in fact, the parents work. Although there are problems of definition (for example, full- or part-time work, job training, job seeking, layoffs), this would be a relatively easy program in which to define standards. As we have seen, however, the goals and purposes of most programs, especially social services programs, are rarely this simple. The goals of most social services programs are rehabilitative and thus very difficult to measure. For example, does the provision of day care strengthen family ties, reduce tension, and generally increase the family's ability to cope? How are these things defined and measured? Are the changes due to day care? Under present theory and knowledge, these questions cannot be readily answered, but unless they can be answered, the performance of a program cannot be objectively evaluated.

Despite the great difficulties in defining accurate standards of performance for all but the most simple programs, there is an irresistible and understandable pressure to develop management and control systems to find out what is going on and how money is being spent. The imposition of these systems has had unfortunate results. Although management control techniques have a history as long as organized government, the "new era" probably dates from the emergence of "systems analysis" or Planning, Programming, and Budget Systems (PPBS) in the mid-1960s. The essential idea behind PPBS was that agency decision making could be controlled through budgeting, which would define and place values on various results and the decisions leading to them, and allow calculation of the cost–benefit ratio of each combination (Sharkansky, 1970, pp. 172–173; Wildavsky, 1974; Sapolsky, 1972). The popularity of PPBS was due to the apparent success with which the Defense Department used systems analysis for its procurement decisions in the early 1960s. By 1965, the Bureau of the Budget imposed PPBS on all government agencies; 5 years later the effort was abandoned by the Office of Management and Budget (Schick, 1973). Many reasons are given for the failure of PPBS, but the principal one of concern here was the inability of many agencies to define and translate social goals into monetary or other quantitative terms (Frederikson, 1974; Waldo, 1972; Chitwood, 1975).

Nevertheless, the search for more accurate and refined evaluation techniques continued (DeWoolfson, 1975). A variety of evaluation techniques were used, the most popular being Management By Objectives (MBO) (Jun, 1976; Havens, 1976), but problems abounded. Evaluation efforts were often not integrated into or accepted by many programs, communication was often faulty, and problems were especially acute among those agencies with diffuse and conflicting goals.[2] In addition, it is to the advantage of field-level workers to maximize their discretion by resisting precise, quantitative definitions of their performance and, under the federal grant-in-aid system, it is more profitable for a state to cover up errors rather than run the risk of having their federal grants reduced for known administrative errors. In short, it is easy enough to collect information, but making sense of it is another matter entirely (Simon, 1973).

Despite the problems in developing sensible management control techniques, by 1970 it was clear that social welfare agencies had little choice but to institute such systems. The General Accounting Office, the Office of Management and Budget, and other congressional and executive offices sought to enhance their oversight role. The future of agency programs often depended on their ability to produce facts and figures and to specify their goals and accomplishments. At the present time there are increased demands for making social welfare agencies more accountable, but— because of the imperfect state of the art, political pressures, and the wide variety of federal, state, and local programs—the type, quality, and effectiveness of evaluation and control programs are very uneven. There are continuing battles over the need to impose reporting systems on programs whose goals, standards, and purposes do not fit or only partially fit the monitoring categories created for them. These struggles have three important consequences.

First, given the current state of the art, it is doubtful whether present management and quality control systems can be relied upon to systematically correct field-level errors or to reduce significantly the need for other client protection mechanisms. This is not to say that a given agency or program does not have an effective supervisory system which has reduced error, but only that the presumption should run the other way. Management systems for social agencies are still crude, and there are a great many reasons why the implementation of such systems has been hindered. As a matter of national policy, one cannot assume the effectiveness of evaluation efforts.

---

[2]On these evaluation efforts see Poland (1974), Horst et al. (1974), Wholey et al. (1970), Kershaw (1970), Levine (1970), Williams (1971), Rivlin (1971), Campbell (1977, pp. 233–261).

Second, the pressure on management to produce facts and figures can distort agency goals and may increase the need for client protections. The distortion effects of statistical controls is a well-documented fact (Blau, 1963). In social service agencies, one of the principal effects, as Newman and Turem (1974) point out, is the substitution of methods for results as the measure of performance. A well-known example involves counseling clients: Because of the difficulties in defining the results of counseling, social service agencies define the effectiveness of their counseling service in terms of numbers of client counseling hours, which is, of course, the method rather than the result. If a given evaluation system stresses the number of persons an agency serves, then the agency will encourage contact with large numbers of clients but the quality of the counseling sessions will be less important. If the monitoring system for an employment training program emphasizes the number of job placements, then the agency will tend merely to place people and not worry whether they retain the jobs. On the other hand, if the monitoring system emphasizes successful job placements, then the employment agency will tend to "cream," that is, to accept and concentrate on only those applicants who have the best chance of succeeding in the employment market anyway. The point is that ill-conceived evaluation systems can seriously warp agency goals to the detriment of the clients.

The third consequence is less obvious but in some respects poses the greatest danger to social service clients. It is the need to gather information and the effect that data-gathering and processing has on the privacy interests of social services clients.

THE INFORMATION-GATHERING PROBLEM

The heart of any management or quality control technique is its data-gathering system. Supervisors have to have information about what decisions are being made, who is receiving or not receiving what kinds of services, for what reasons, from what organizations, and with what results. Without such information, there is little or no basis for measuring and evaluating agency performance. Yet obtaining the necessary information is a difficult task for a number of reasons. The first difficulty is related to the question of standards and involves a decision about what kind of information is needed for what purposes. For example, if day care is to be granted only to working parents, then the employment of the parent is the measure of performance, and information can be gathered to document whether or not the day care slot was properly allocated. On the other hand, if day care is to be allocated for rehabilitative purposes, the information-gathering process is far more difficult because there is no agreed-upon measure of rehabilitation.

Even assuming that the proper measures of performance can be agreed upon, the nature of the information itself poses difficulties. Employment data are objective and easily documented by employer records. Rehabilitative data, on the other hand, are not of this nature but consist primarily of case records that are summary accounts giving the subjective opinion of the treating caseworker as to whether or not the rehabilitative goals have been met. Not only is such information not quantifiable or objective (as, for example, an employment record is), but it is written by the official who will subsequently be evaluated on the basis of that same report. The potential for abuse is obvious. Supervisors and controllers are, of course, aware of this weakness and sometimes have independent evaluators investigate the decisions, but this is a costly procedure. It is precisely the difficulty of obtaining reliable information on rehabilitative goals that drives management to search for short-cut indicators of performance which can be easily collected and verified. But the result of this pressure is to obtain data that do not accurately measure performance goals, or, more likely, that substitute methods for results and quantity for quality.

Efforts to devise and implement data-gathering systems can seriously affect the privacy interests of clients. Once information seekers move beyond the easily verifiable documentary evidence (for example, employment records) into more personal, subjective rehabilitative issues, data are needed on a variety of personal matters. In order to make the discussion concrete, consider how a standard social services case—a family seeking counseling about their marital and parent–child problems—illustrates some of the difficulties of gathering information. If the family is seeking services from a Title XX agency, they must provide financial eligibility information such as income, other resources, and the number of working children living at home. Historical information is also needed: marital histories, personal and psychological data, health and mental health records, school records, employment history, and previous contacts with other agencies. In family therapy, information in any of these areas might be relevant to the family's problems. A poor employment record of the principal breadwinner might be reflected in identity problems at home. Failures in home management might be causing tension among family members. A tension-ridden home life might be affecting school performance or relations with neighbors. If the family's problems are relatively simple and straightforward, they may be alleviated by obtaining better housing, or by having a teen-age family member move out, or by having the wife get a job. But in more complex situations, the social worker will have to explore sensitive issues such as personal communications, sex, drug abuse, alcoholism, crime, nonsupport, adultery, and poor work records. As we noted in Chapter 1, there are no clearly defined theories specifying relationships between variables in family difficulties; under the prevailing social work theory, the social worker is to explore underlying problems to deal with causes rather than symptoms. As a theoretical matter, relevancy is hard to define; operationally, the social worker and sometimes the client decide on a case-by-case basis what areas are relevant and what areas are too far afield in building the historical record of the family.

In addition to gathering the family history, there is also a need for so-called process data. One type of process data is a record of quantifiable behavioral activity, such as the number of professional hours the social worker has spent with various members of the family, the length of the sessions, their location, and the number and type of contacts with other agencies. Another kind of process data deals with the interaction between the family and the social worker and the family's reactions to the relationship. This is the heart of counseling: How does the social worker help the family explore the nature of its problems? How are symptoms and causes identified? What treatment is best? How skillful is the social worker in helping the family arrive at self-realization? Does the social worker manipulate or threaten the family? Under what circumstances does the family ask for and receive valuable hard services, and what, if anything, do they have to do in return?

A third kind of necessary information is data on the results of the counseling. Again, the lack of theory combined with lack of scientific controls destroys a definition of relevancy. If a child stops misbehaving after the family has been counseled, is it because of the therapy or because the child has a new homeroom teacher at school or because an older sibling moved out? Is the home better managed because of an improvement in parent–child relations or because the husband changed his job or because of the skilled advice of the social worker? Since there is no way of controlling for results, one is reduced to clinical hunches.

The type of information gathered about the family in the example above is by no means exhaustive, and one can easily imagine family circumstances that would require other kinds of information. The range of relevant information depends on how the problem is conceived and defined. Psychiatrically oriented social work theory conceives of family problems as being deep, complex issues, which extend far beyond the immediate family members. Other social services are far more limited. For example, according to the Wisconsin Social Services Manual, "chore services" are routine household services "usually done by family members to enable individuals to remain in their own homes when unable to perform such tasks themselves [State of Wisconsin, 1977, chap. 6, p. A, 2.e]." Installing weather stripping or removing snow for an elderly, infirm couple on Supplementary Security Income would present a fairly simple data gathering problem for the purposes of management and quality control; financial eligibility has already been determined, and medical reports would satisfy the physical disability documentation. For a relatively simple, clear-cut service, the information problem is much more easily managed.

Another question is how the information is obtained. Much information is documentary and can be obtained merely by examining the case file, which will show whether the social worker has gathered the required historical documentation, such as school and employment records and marital history. Independent checks would have to be made to see if community and agency contacts were followed up, since the absence of records documenting contacts can mean either no contacts or sloppy casework. Obtaining this kind of external historical information is relatively painless; it usually involves only leg work or telephoning by the social worker. There are, however, important issues of privacy involved. The client, for example, might not want juvenile or drug abuse records disclosed to the social services agency. This issue is discussed more fully later in this chapter.

A much more serious problem arises when the family must supply the necessary historical information. Members of the family are approaching the social services agency about sensitive issues; there most likely is controversy among family members themselves as to whether they need help, where they should go, the value of the sessions, the motives of the social worker, and so forth. Obtaining internal family information is not a costless exercise. The need of the social worker to ask detailed questions, to administer batteries of tests, and to inquire into community contacts can easily raise barriers to a successful professional relationship. Members of the family might well feel that their privacy is being invaded. If there is a record of deviant or criminal behavior, the family may suffer embarrassment, which can chill its willingness to participate.

The social worker might also resent having to obtain the detailed information required by supervisory controllers; not only can such questioning serve to sour the professional relationship, but it also makes the social worker more amenable to supervisory control and discipline. While social workers have maximum control over information generated in the privacy of therapy sessions, they have far less control over information from outside sources. The more detailed this outside information must be, the more chance the social worker has of making an error. If, for example, so-cial—psychological tests must be administered, the social worker becomes vulnerable to an evaluator who says that the tests were improperly given or evaluated or were not properly utilized. Thus, it is in the social worker's interest to keep information gathering to a minimum and to collect only those data which he can keep within his control. By so doing, the social worker serves his professional interest as well as his bureaucratic, career interest, and at the same time makes his job less burdensome.

In addition to internal historical information from clients, agencies may require outside verification. From time to time, regulations require that certain kinds of client-supplied information be verified by independent sources. Thus banks, employers, schools, the courts, the police, and other social agencies might have to be contacted to verify client information. For the reasons given earlier, verification is burdensome to the social worker, can work at cross purposes to the main job of establishing client relation-ships, and can prove offensive to the client.

Obtaining information about the social worker—client therapy sessions presents even more difficulties. The standard method is to review the written reports of the social worker, which purport to summarize what happened. That is the cheapest method of obtaining information, but, for obvious reasons, can be quite unreliable. The social worker, in this pos-ture, has the greatest control over the information that the supervisors will receive. Another method would be to reinterview the client to get his version of the interaction. This method is expensive and also presents reliability problems; the client's perception of what happened, like the social worker's, may or may not be accurate. Sessions could be video-taped. However, in addition to the expense, there are problems of prior disclosure, privacy issues, and possible chilling effects.

The example of family counseling illustrates the close connection be-tween the definition of a social services task and the consequent problems of data gathering and management control. If the social services task is defined simply, with a minimum of eligibility conditions and outcome mea-sures, such as the snow removal for the SSI family, then obtaining the information for management control is relatively simple. But this is the rare case. To the extent that Title XX services are stated in terms of rehabilita-tion goals, the range of relevancy for information gathering and evaluation purposes expands enormously. Day care, for example, is not simply available to allow a mother to work; rather it is "for promotion of social, health and emotional wellbeing through opportunities for companionship, self-education, and other developmental activities." This expanded definition of purposes increases the range of discretion of social workers to use day care for traditional social work rehabilitation objectives, and thus the problems involved in data gathering and evaluation will begin to resemble those in the family therapy example. But because of data gathering and evaluation difficulties, there is a tendency to reduce evaluations to readily quantifiable measures, which, as Newman and Turem (1974) point out, become inputs rather than outputs. If one cannot find out what is happening in the therapy session or how it affects outcomes, at least one can count the number of social work hours spent with various family members. Such quantifiable measures, however, will not tell supervisors what is happening or what is being accomplished.

DATA-GATHERING ISSUES UNDER TITLE XX

Under Title XX, there is pressure to develop an extensive, penetrating data-gathering operation to cover a wide range of information about families and individuals who use the services. The situation is greatly complicated by the fact that Title XX is an open-ended statute that allows for the provision of a large number of social services so long as they fit within the diffuse statutory goal of rehabilitation. A further problem is that the administration of Title XX is highly decentralized; it is a revenue-sharing statute designed to maximize state discretion and flexibility in the expenditure of monies. In addition, many social services are provided by private agencies that contract with state Title XX agencies. Thus, the normally difficult task of keeping track of the activities of a social service agency is compounded by the decentralized administration of Title XX and by the fact that the states have found loopholes in Title XX that allow them to redefine traditional state services to qualify for Title XX money.

For all these reasons, it is understandable why HEW, in funding Title XX, is concerned with creating an accurate information-gathering system in order to establish effective monitoring and quality control. The regulations that were initially issued to implement Title XX purported to accomplish these objectives. Originally, state Title XX agencies were required to maintain a basic data file on each individual recipient. This meant that all Title XX social services recipients, no matter what the service provided, were listed in a central state data file. The purpose of the file was to overcome at least some of the problems of monitoring a decentralized administrative structure; it would provide uniform data on all recipients in one easily accessible place.

In addition to containing "identifying information about the recipient," the file had to include information about the person's eligibility, the services provided, the goals to which the services were directed, and the name of the provider agency. The eligibility information was very detailed. It had to include all sources of income and had to be signed under penalty of perjury. Moreover, eligibility could not be determined solely on the basis of the application; there had to be documentation about every source of income, and eligibility had to be redetermined every 6 months. The amount of detail required for eligibility was not required for other categories of information. The agencies were allowed considerable discretion to decide how much specificity is required about the individual recipient, the services provided, and the goals of the services. HEW or the state Title XX agency could require extensive, penetrating information about the family members and their environment, or they could limit the amount of information required. In addition to the material on the recipients themselves the data files contained information on the agencies providing services. In this way, the supervising agency (either the state Title XX agency or HEW) could more easily check on agency performance as well as on client fraud.

The regulations concerning basic data files produced a great deal of protest from Legal Services lawyers, and litigation was instituted against HEW. There were a number of objections to the regulations, the most serious being that the regulations constituted a massive invasion of privacy of social services recipients. The great amount of eligibility information required was considered unnecessary and stigmatizing. There was also fear that recipients would be required to disclose information that would be embarrassing and harmful in other situations—for example, information about drug abuse, nonsupport, criminality or delinquency, and mental health. It was feared that sensitive information about clients would impair confidential relationships, would erect barriers to the use of social services, and, despite disclaimers and prohibitions in the regulations, would find its way to other agencies dealing with the recipients. There were also objections that the regulations were unauthorized by the Title XX statute and contravened the purpose of state autonomy, and that the information system mandated was costly and burdensome to the states and would impede the development of Title XX. However, the main thrust of the poverty lawyers' attack was on the potential harm to the recipients.

Because of the strong protest, HEW modified the eligibility determination rules in March 1976. Two months later HEW withdrew the requirement that the states establish a basic data file, "including the unique identifier," for each individual recipient. The perjury penalty provision has also been eliminated; currently, the applicant merely certifies that the information is correct. The states are free to establish other application processes, including a self-declaration method, and to vary the methods for different kinds of services. This means that the requirement of independent verification for all eligibility factors has been dropped; it also means that simplified eligibility can be used for particular services. The states are required, however, to establish monitoring systems for whatever provisions they establish.

None of the issues raised by information systems have been resolved. In a curious turnabout, welfare rights lawyers, at least under the Nixon administration, argued for state discretion vis-à-vis the federal government; in almost all of the prior welfare rights controversies, the lawyers had attacked the states and sought the support of HEW or other federal law. State discretion for information systems only spreads the issues; it does not solve them. The difference is that the states are not required to establish centralized, uniform data-gathering systems. The basic problems of monitoring and quality control remain unsolved. After the experience of the Nixon administration, the need for supervision of expenditures is stronger than ever since the federal government wants to continue to use revenue sharing on a program basis.[3]

What, then, are the issues raised by centralized information-gathering systems? In the family therapy example, the range and extent of information relevant to a management quality control system was discussed. Why does the gathering of this information cause so much concern?

In the last decade several scholars have called attention to the invasions of privacy that occur as the result of information-gathering systems. Although their concerns and perspectives vary, they are basically in agreement that the privacy problem began with federal government programs in areas such as Social Security, health, urban planning, and home financing, which had a specific interest in acquiring dossiers on individuals. Technological innovations in data processing made it easier and cheaper to store and analyze quantities of data as the desire to obtain more information about individuals and their environment grew. Within a short time, information retrieval and storage became a massive industry.

---

[3]On the growing use of integrated information systems (i.e., single storage place for information that can be used for several different welfare programs), see Congressional Research Service (1977, pp. 151–163).

Given the cost of initial data gathering, the most economic approach was to obtain the information and decide later on its application. Under Title XX, with its lack of relevancy standards and its wide variety of services to a broad segment, the tendency was to cast a wide data-gathering net, store the information, and use particular data as the need arose, storing the unused information for future use.

The danger to privacy is that this information can be disseminated to a wider audience than the client originally consented to and who could use it to the detriment of the client. Inaccurate information may be given to a wider audience stemming from computer malfunction, from intrusions into the data processing system, from transcription errors, or from personnel oversight or misuse. Controls for most of these problems exist, but they are expensive. Formerly, problems of erroneous information were more limited because data files were local and machine technology did not allow the information to be widely diffused. Today, data gathered for one purpose may be made available to public and private agencies for other purposes; improper data may be used in and out of context, and inappropriate subjective labeling may follow a person via his computer files. Each of these criticisms only touches on the issues, and only the beginnings of control have appeared. The assembly and consolidation of personal dossier information is increasing with the steady proliferation of data banks.

The federal government is the largest user of machine-readable data files on individuals. The Census Bureau, the Social Security Administration, and the Internal Revenue Service produce more than 600 million annual reports.[4] There is a strong push to encourage states to create central files on social welfare recipients (Congressional Research Service, 1977). Social, economic, and environmental planning are becoming increasingly dependent on statistical information. Despite the growing use of computer data, the federal government's efforts lack coherence and direction. Many agencies work at cross-purposes with other agencies; there is much duplication; some agencies have strict confidentiality rules and cannot share their information. In the 1960s, the Bureau of Management and the Budget attempted to rationalize all of the federal government's information-gathering activities by proposing a single federal statistical center called the National Data Center. Proponents of the center claimed that it would make more data available to both government and outside researchers, reduce the unit cost of data gathering, facilitate wider use of

---

[4]On IRS computers, see *The Washington Post* (1977).

more variables in analysis, reduce duplication, promote standardization, and provide a data processing pool for all information-handling agencies. The proposal produced a storm of criticism from Congress, the press, and others who attacked the accompanying reports for maximizing the efficiency aspects and paying little attention to the protections of individual privacy. For example, despite protestations, it was later admitted that there had to be individual identification at the center. Ironically, during the course of the debate about the proposed center, opponents began to view the haphazard, decentralized federal information-gathering system not in terms of inefficiency but as a protection for individuals "against the compilation of extensive government dossiers on every citizen."

Although the plan was eventually withdrawn, little has been done to protect the privacy of individuals who give information to the government. The penchant of government agencies for continually expanding their data-gathering activities continues. Instead of having one National Data Center under legislative control, we are now witnessing the expansion of several national data centers. Federal agencies have large quantities of data about individuals as well as statutory authority to share that information. The General Services Administration, for example, has authority to provide for interagency cooperative use of facilities and equipment. As of 1970, approximately 20 federal agencies were either operating time-sharing computers or establishing them. The information-gathering agencies are pushing toward greater coordination and exchange. This process is encouraged by two powerful agencies more concerned with governmental efficiency than sensitivity to privacy—the Office of Management and Budget and the General Accounting Office. The continued effort is to increase the efficiency of government data gathering. Finally, there is no reason to assume that the tendency toward more refined information gathering at the federal government level is not also present at the state and local levels and in the private sector.

An HEW report of the Secretary's Advisory Committee on Automated Personal Data Systems, entitled *Records, Computers, and the Rights of Citizens* and issued in 1973, shared the concern about the dangerous effect of centralized government data-gathering systems on the privacy of individuals. The committee had been appointed to "analyze the consequences of using computers to keep records about people" and was instructed to pay "particular attention to the dangers implicit in the drift of the Social Security number toward becoming an all-purpose personal identifier [U.S. Department of Health, Education, and Welfare, 1973, p. 4]." After reviewing the growth and development of computerized information systems and the dangers to personal privacy, the committee recommended five basic principles as "safeguard requirements" for automated personal data systems. In addition to full disclosure of such systems, the safeguards called for mechanisms by which individuals could find out their dossier information and how it was being used, ways they could prevent information obtained for one purpose from being used for another without consent, means to correct information, and a requirement that organizations gathering personal information assure reliability and prevent the unauthorized use of data. The committee opposed the establishment of a standard universal identifier as well as the drift toward using the Social Security number for this purpose. In the committee's words, "A persistent source of public concern is that the Social Security number will be used to assemble dossiers on individuals from fragments of data in widely dispersed systems" which will deepen "the anxieties of a public already suffused with concern about surveillance [U.S. Department of Health, Education, and Welfare, 1973, p. 5]."[5]

---

[5]Concern about the growth and dangers of the dossier society, the increase in distrust of the federal government, and the difficulties that citizens were encountering in obtaining information from government led to the passage of a series of statutes designed to increase access to information and to protect privacy. These statutes included the Freedom of Information Act, its subsequent amendments, and the Privacy Act of 1974, which purports to enact the principles of the HEW Advisory Committee on Automated Personal Data Systems report discussed in the text.

There are many reasons why the Privacy Act of 1974 will not solve most of the problems of the dossier society, especially as these problems pertain to social services clients. The act applies only to the federal government; thus, it is inapplicable to all the state, local, and private agencies that administer Title XX programs and collect data. The overwhelming majority of Title XX recipients will be totally unaware of the act's existence; notice is provided only in the *Federal Register*, hardly a document that the average citizen is aware of. A person has access only to his own file; he has no access to other people's files even though his name appears in those files. The person who requests the information has to bear the cost of the request. In addition, numerous agencies are exempt from the act, principally law enforcement agencies and other agencies that do some investigative work for law enforcement purposes. As two knowledgeable commentators remarked on this particular exemption, "An irony of the Privacy Act is that it exempts precisely those agencies and kinds of records systems the abuses of which generated much of the very concern that led to passage of the Act [Hanus and Relyea, 1976, p. 586]." These are only some of the more obvious problems under the statute. In addition, the statute is poorly drafted, contains serious ambiguities, and is inconsistent with the Freedom of Information Act. It is reported that there is much confusion among agencies about compliance.

Thus, even assuming good faith on the part of administrators, the Privacy Act will not be of much help to most Title XX clients. But there is no reason to assume good faith on the part of administrators, who in the past have generally shown a remarkable lack of sensitivity to privacy interests. Since the risk of apprehension and penalty under the act is so slight, one would expect life to continue much as before. For discussions of the Privacy Act of 1974, in addition to Hanus and Relyea, see Shurn and Parker (1976), and Comments (1976).

It is against this background that the opposition formed to the HEW Title XX regulations that required detailed recipient information and the establishment of central data bank files. Lawyers who have worked with juvenile delinquents, children in trouble, criminals, and other adults in various forms of delinquent or socially marginal behavior are well aware of the dangers of the dissemination of supposedly confidential information. It is not an exaggeration to say that only the client lacks access to his file. The giving of detailed information, as I outlined in the family therapy example, increases the vulnerability of the clients without giving them any benefits. The information, they feel, is not necessary for the provision of the service and is only required to further encourage the government's appetite for information.

As already indicated, the problems of information gathering are not simple. Both HEW and the states have an interest in monitoring the expenditures of funds, controlling client fraud, making sure that tax dollars are spent for legitimate purposes. In order to accomplish these objectives, they must have access to a certain amount of information. Even though HEW may have been temporarily sidetracked in its efforts to obtain the information, there are strong incentives at the state level to keep on top of Title XX funds.

At the present time, the situation on centralized data gathering on Title XX clients is still in flux. To what extent are states developing information systems, and for what purposes? Will the states make this information available to HEW? The states have an interest in nondisclosure to the federal government to prevent penalties from being imposed for rates of error; HEW, of course, has the opposite incentive, and we can expect a struggle over record keeping, information gathering, and disclosure between the states and HEW. There will be continuing incentives for the state social welfare agencies, including the Title XX agency, to cooperate with other information systems within the state, including law enforcement, mental health, and schools. Like the defeat of the proposed National Data Center, the withdrawal of HEW regulations, which would have provided a visible, uniform system, more amenable to controls for client protection, may be a Pyrrhic victory. States' rights in welfare have never been regarded as the route to client protection. At the present time, the threat to client privacy through information systems has been decentralized to 50 states, but the problems of providing information for management and quality control have not been solved.

6

Structural Alternatives

As I have discussed, two of the principal sources of discretion are the vagueness and ambiguity in the language of rules and the nature of the bureaucratic structure. Are there ways in which discretion can be reduced by changing the language in rules and bureaucratic structures? This chapter examines two structural methods of reducing discretion: modification of the character of rules and reorganization of delivery systems.

RULES

Rules are usually considered to be the opposite of discretion. At least in theory, a clearly stated, specific rule confines the official's choice to that which is commanded by the rule. The dichotomy between rules and discretion is useful but should not be taken literally. Elimination of all discretion by a rule is rare, and in a great many situations it is probably undesirable as well. Rather, the focus is on degrees; more or less rule specificity produces more or less discretion. Rules are commands, but they may or may not be obeyed; they may be used as threats or as bargaining chips for other courses of action. It is a common characteristic of administrative

117

systems that informal behavior patterns grow up and sometimes assume more importance than the formal rule structure.[1] This system of "informal discretion" is discussed in Chapter 1.

It is generally thought that specific rules favor the client, especially the social services client who is relatively poor and who lacks the resources to bargain effectively with the agency. Specific rules disclose information about what the social work officials are expected to do; they maximize client protection because the client or his advocate, when confronting the agency, can open the manual, point out the rule, and demand that the agency follow it. But specific rules can also hurt clients. Specific rules exclude as well as include. Rules are a forecast of the future; they attempt to envisage many different future situations and to specify how these situations should be handled. Both in theory and in practice this is an impossible task, and the difference between a carefully worked-out rule and a bad rule is the amount of error produced, not whether there is any error at all. In social services, there will always be situations that ought to be covered by the rules and would have been covered had anyone thought about them. Specific rules that have teeth and are binding on lower-level officials come from an authoritative source and usually are not easily or quickly amended; therefore, they inevitably produce hardship cases. From the client's perspective, there is a dilemma about the character of rules; there is a trade-off between the protection afforded by specific rules and the hardships produced by their inability to provide for all possible contingencies.

In some instances specific rules are beneficial to social workers; a clear rule allows them to make quick decisions, which make their job easier. But, on the whole, social workers favor rules that authorize the exercise of discretion. Discretion is inherent in the concept of professionalism, which encompasses the ability and authority to act according to reasoned, expert judgment. Specific rules for the allocation of services have the opposite effect; they deprofessionalize social workers and turn them into clerks. This point, of course, has not gone unnoticed, and those who have argued for more simplified welfare and social service systems have counted as one of the benefits a reduction in the need for trained social workers, an argument not likely to find favor with social workers (Sinfield, 1970).

Discretionary rules are important to social workers for other reasons. Since social workers allocate scarce resources according to a casework plan, discretionary rules allow them to exercise their judgment as to which

---

[1]See, for example, Macaulay (1966) on informal versus formal rules.

clients can best use what services. If particular services are of great importance to a family, then the ability to control the allocation of these desired
goods gives the social worker increased leverage over the family. If the
family wants the service, they will listen carefully to what the social worker
has to say.

A third reason why social workers favor discretionary rules is that it
allows them to control information about the decisions they make. Specific
rules are usually more amenable to statistical monitoring than are rules that
provide for discretionary judgments, especially since the primary source of
information about the latter is the case file prepared by the social worker.
As stated in the last chapter, control of information is the key to supervision; if the social worker can retain control of the information on which his
decisions are based, he can greatly hamper effective supervision.

Routinization versus Discretion

The different consequences of specific versus discretionary rules are best
illustrated by considering some examples.[2] Public housing can be allocated
in at least two ways: on a first-come, first-served basis within clearly defined
categories, or as part of a general family rehabilitation plan. In the first
instance, the criteria for obtaining housing are relatively routine and clear-
cut. Does the family meet the financial eligibility requirements? Do the
people seeking the housing unit meet the definition of a family? Do unmarried adults constitute a family? Are non-nuclear-family members (i.e.,
nephews, nieces, grandparents) properly part of the family? Under such a
system, apartments can be allocated with a minimum of administrative
cost, and the rule appears to be equitable; within rationally related
categories such as family size, all families are treated equally.

If housing is allocated as part of a general rehabilitative program—for
example, as a means of preventing family stress or deterioration—the
administrative and discretionary problems multiply.[3] Because there is no
precise, generally recognized concept of family disorganization or its causes
and no agreement as to what degree of intrafamilial conflict constitutes
disorganization, there is no way to predict in advance which families will
qualify for rehabilitative housing. The test is not only whether the family

---

[2]For an excellent discussion of the trade-off between discretion and rules, see Jowell (1975,
chaps. 1, 5).

[3]For a discussion of the British system of allocating public housing for rehabilitation purposes, see Handler (1973, pp. 72–74).

has fallen below some minimum level of deviance, but also whether, in the social worker's judgment, the family will be helped by obtaining new housing. Under such a system, therefore, administrative discretion is maximized and client protection is minimized, but special cases can be taken into account. Under the more routinized system, which is more easily administered and seemingly more equitable, special cases of hardship often cannot be accommodated, but client protection is greater because of the existence of relatively objective rules.

Another serious, albeit hidden, problem of the routinized system is that the very existence of rules often affects behavior in unintended ways. Rules often assume equal information, which, of course, does not exist; some families will not get on the list because they are unaware of its existence or think that they do not qualify. There are also incentive effects. As long as income eligibility rules exist, for example, families have a disincentive to increase their earnings because increased wages will mean loss of public housing. Similarly, eligibility based on the composition of the family may foster the shifting of adults and children within and among families, often to the detriment of the familial relationship, in order to comply with eligibility standards. Thus seemingly simple and neutral nondiscretionary rules may have various side effects on social behavior, which must be taken into account.

As complicated and difficult as the allocation of housing can become, the dilemmas are far more acute with money. As we know, a persistent criticism of the AFDC program is that the individualized grant, tailored to meet the family's needs, has resulted in a highly complicated, discretionary, unpredictable, and error-prone system. The reform impetus is to replace AFDC with a simplified, uniform income-maintenance system, such as a negative income tax, demogrant, or some variation. Financial eligibility would be simplified and fairly clear-cut; many of the other conditions and qualifications that presently exist in welfare would be eliminated. The effort is to obtain uniformity rather than individualized treatment. It is felt that more justice, in the sense of equality of treatment, will be accomplished by a nondiscretionary system.

A major problem with a uniform income-maintenance system is that some provision has to be made for individual hardship cases. Unless there are considerable changes in the redistribution of income in the United States, a uniform income-maintenance system will not be pegged at a generous level. For many individuals and families, such a system will be inadequate; they will not be able to provide for emergencies, such as fire or the temporary loss of a job, or for special but chronic situations, such as the need for a certain diet. Unless provision is made for these special circumstances, families with low incomes may be forced into even more dire circumstances.

The British Experience

The experience in Great Britain provides an interesting example of the dilemmas posed by a uniform income-maintenance plan with a discretionary monetary safety valve. After World War II, Great Britain established a nationwide, uniform income-maintenance system which, along with health insurance, was designed to provide a security floor for the entire population; the policy emphasis was on uniform treatment rather than on individual needs. It was felt that the average family could cope so long as basic security was provided by health insurance and a national income-maintenance program. It was quickly recognized, however, that social services were needed to help families who still had difficulty coping. At first services were offered to these "families at risk" through various statutory programs: housing, health, education, welfare, and child protection. Then, by the early 1960s, a general preventive service was established in the Children's Departments to promote the welfare of children by diminishing the likelihood of family breakup or the institutionalization of children. The Children's Departments were authorized to provide "assistance in kind or, in exceptional circumstances, in cash [Handler, 1973, pp. 62, 72–74]."

The enabling legislation for the Children's Department preventive service, and the standards for giving emergency cash, contained very few guidelines. Money was only to be given in "exceptional" circumstances, but what did that mean? Money has a quality that distinguishes it from other hard goods at the disposal of social services departments. Housing and other hard goods are rationed by supply and carry their own limitations on use; if a family wants something from the social service agency but is for some reason ineligible, it is a simple matter to deny the request. But money is far more flexible; it can be used for a multitude of purposes, and if enough people know about it, has a runaway quality. The British supervising agency, the Home Office, was plainly worried about the runaway qualities of money and, in its regulations, cautioned local agencies to avoid giving the impression that access to this resource was a claim of right or that it could be used as a supplement to the regular income-maintenance system. But characteristically, neither the Home Office nor the local agencies were able to come up with definitions of what constituted a "family at risk" and what "exceptional" circumstances meant. The decision about whether or not to grant money was left to the agency and Child Care Officers' (CCO) discretion.

The availability of discretionary money posed serious problems for the CCO. The availability of money could destroy professional goals of rehabilitation. Why, for example, should a family save and pay its bills if it could run to the local agency and have the bills paid? How were the agencies to prevent people in the community from coming in and demanding their fair share of the discretionary money? The agencies tried to develop two strategies for the handling of the money. The first was not to advertise its availability. People had to ask for the money; thus those most in need might not receive it because they were ignorant of its availability. The other strategy was to use the money only as part of a casework plan. Failure to pay bills was viewed as a presenting problem, which enabled the agency to examine the total family situation. As one CCO stated, "It is quite rare . . . when a family is in arrears that there is only one thing wrong—they are usually a multi-problem family [Quoted in Handler, 1973, p. 66]."

The British social workers varied widely in their administration of discretionary money. Some workers insisted on real desperation before any money was given and, even then, it was viewed as unprofessional or "bad" for the family to be given a grant outright. In such cases, bills were paid directly to the creditor. Other social workers used their financial power to become more directly involved in the affairs of the family; they assumed the role of family budget officers and rent collectors. But other social workers, contrary to the instructions of the Home Office, allowed families to draw upon the discretionary money for recurring bills and thus use the resource as a fairly regular supplement to the income maintenance system.

The CCOs were well aware of the power that the discretionary money gave them, and they did not shrink from using that power. Prior to the new legislation, many of them had already been involved in budgeting, rent collecting, and other kinds of management. Now they had new leverage over their clients, and the workers were quite forthright in insisting on various kinds of behavioral changes before giving any money. In some instances, after repeated failures, the agency would refuse to pay rent arrears and would allow a family to be evicted or to have its electricity shut off before paying the bills. The granting of nonemergency requests for financial help was often based on whether a family could "make a relationship" with the Children's Department.[4]

---

[4]For a recent study of the continued troubles of this program, see Hill and Laing (1978). The major income-maintenance welfare program, Supplementary Benefits, is also experiencing great difficulty with the rise of discretionary benefits in what is supposed to be a relatively routinized, flat-grant program. See Supplementary Benefits Commission (1976).

It would be a mistake to dismiss the British experience with discretionary social services money as heavy-handed, unprofessional paternalism. In the departments that were studied, the staff members were highly professional, educated, sympathetic social workers who enjoyed a national reputation. When interviewed, they were not defensive about their methods; rather, they emphasized that they were dealing with families with severe problems, that their job was to keep the families together and, as is usually the case with public social services departments, that they were under constant pressure to get the work done.

The lesson to be learned from the British experience, as well as from the housing example, has been a repeated theme: The inclusion of vague statutory language creates discretionary authority, and if policymakers want to control field-level decisions and maximize client protection, then individualized treatment and professional discretion must be sacrificed. The differences are matters of degree, but one quickly moves along the continuum from routinization to discretion. The statutory purposes of Title XX itself illustrate the differences in the continuum. The first purpose of Title XX is job related: to achieve or maintain "economic self-support to prevent, reduce, or eliminate dependency." If the statute stopped at that point, then presumably all Title XX services would have to be job related, and unless an applicant could show job-related need, he or she would not be eligible. Thus, for example, day care would not be available for a mother who needed some relief during the day because of emotional problems. The second purpose of Title XX is to achieve or maintain "self-sufficiency," which somehow is different from mere economic self-sufficiency. Presumably, under the second purpose, the mother would be eligible for non-job-related day care, but the statutory language is unclear. In any event, the third statutory purpose opens the door completely: It is to prevent or remedy "neglect, abuse, or exploitation of children and adults unable to protect their own interests," or to "preserve, rehabilitate, or reunite families." Like the statute governing the British Social Services Department, Title XX is completely open, nonspecific, and entirely discretionary.[5]

Wisconsin Social Services

State services mirror this approach. In Wisconsin, for example, day care is available "for the promotion of social, health, and emotional well-being

---

[5]On the difficulties in drafting specific rules and guidelines for social service programs, including Title XX, see Derthick (1976).

through opportunities for companionship, self-education and other developmental activities [State of Wisconsin, 1977, p. 19]." From the professional point of view, this is a good rule. Management will have great difficulty in supervising the allocation of day care; on the other hand, if the top bureaucracy is more interested in expanding the use of the service than in monitoring it, the rule is useful since it provides no real limitations. Since day care is not limited (except to families with young children), the bureaucracy can expand the demand for it and then use the increased demand to request more funding. At the same time, it would be difficult for federal auditors to claim that a day care grant is erroneous. For each social service item the choices are clear. The purposes to be served by the services have to be thought out in terms of administrative consequences to the clients, to the social workers, and to the supervisors.

Take, for example, the Wisconsin provision of chore services. These are defined as "the performance of household tasks, essential shopping, and unskilled or semiskilled home maintenance tasks usually done by family members to enable individuals to remain in their own homes when unable to perform such tasks themselves. Activities include but are not limited to installing weather stripping, repairing furniture, minor painting, cutting grass, and clearing walkways of snow and leaves [State of Wisconsin, 1977, p. 19]." What does this mean? One interpretation is that services are limited to those who, because of temporary or permanent disability, are unable to perform those services themselves.

However, the Wisconsin regulations do not limit the service in this way. If they did, then there would be a fairly clear rule that would maximize client rights, limit social worker discretion, and be fairly susceptible to quality control. In addition to financial eligibility, documentary medical records could be required. If the regulation were expanded to include the provision of services for nonphysical disabilities, then discretion would be broadened, clients would have less protection, and quality control would become more difficult. For example, the regulation could require certification from medical or psychological professionals that the recipient is mentally ill and thus not able to do the tasks. But it is doubtful that a chore service regulation would require this type of formality, since the costs of the determination would clearly exceed the value of the service. What is more likely is that chore services would be available if the Title XX social worker himself determined that the client was unable to perform the tasks. At this point, the discretion of the social worker to decide eligibility becomes very great, and client rights diminish accordingly; furthermore, the client is not likely to appeal the denial of this kind of service; she will just suffer. Quality control also becomes more difficult because the eligibility determination cannot ordinarily be measured. The delivery of the service can still be measured, but delivery is not synonymous with results; it is only a means toward rehabilitation and not an end in itself. The controllers will be restricted to the case file which, as has been pointed out, will have been prepared by the social worker. For items of this nature, it is doubtful whether it is worthwhile for the supervising agency to conduct independent investigations.

If chore services are made part of the casework plan, then eligibility includes not only nonphysical disability, but also the willingness and ability of the client, in the language of the profession, to enter into a relationship, to see the reality of her situation, and to use the service to help herself. There are many situations where this sort of mundane service has proved very effective in helping families. Indeed, the foundations of the preventive service in Great Britain started with the work of the Pacifist Family Services during World War II.[6] These social workers would seek out and work with on a daily basis the most disorganized, poverty-stricken bombed-out families in England. The specific philosophy of the social workers was that literally doing the household chores with the family would rehabilitate the family by not only showing them and helping them with their daily tasks, but also by gaining their confidence and providing them with an example.

Thus, even the most mundane services have been used by social workers as an effective tool in family therapy. If chore services are used in this manner, then we are at the other end of the discretion−rights continuum. As with discretionary counseling, or money, or the other examples given, eligibility for chore services is completely within the discretionary evaluation of the social worker, subject to his opinion as to whether it furthers the casework plan. In such cases, client rights are minimal and clients become dependent on the social worker to the extent that the client needs and wants the particular service or wants to preserve a continuing relationship with the social worker. Quality control is converted to measuring the cost of the service rather than its delivery. The controllers can count the number, kind, and cost of the chore services delivered, but the expected result of the casework plan, of which the service is only one part, is not susceptible to scientific evaluation (see Newman and Turem, 1974).

The drafters of a chore service regulation thus have fairly clear choices; the trade-offs, costs, and benefits of each of the alternatives have been

---

[6]The work of the Pacifist Service Units is described in Stephens (1945).

specified. The Wisconsin regulation purportedly does not make any of these choices; as stated above, chore services are merely supposed to be available to allow a person to remain in his home. But, of course, this regulation does make a choice; by not deciding, the drafters of the regulation have delegated the choice to the local public and to private Title XX agencies. These agencies decide how chore services will be used; moreover, they will allocate chore services according to rules and practices which, for the most part, will never be written down. Patterns of behavior will be learned only from hints in the case files, or from what the social workers and their immediate supervisors choose to disclose. In Wisconsin, the administration of this seemingly mundane service not only will be discretionary but also will be hidden from outside view.

The Wisconsin Title XX Final Comprehensive Social Services Plan lists 22 services that it intends to offer. Of these, at least 7 are services that one would consider central to professional social work casework; that is, they make no sense unless part of a casework plan. They include adoption, counseling, court services, diagnosis and evaluation, planning placement and supervision, protective payment services, and special living arrangements. There are other listed services that are not necessarily part of a casework plan, but the regulations provide that they should be. These include day care, day services, education and training, and recreation. Here, a choice has been made. Recreation could be provided merely for its own sake, eligibility could be minimally stated, outcomes could be measured by the number and kind of participants and activities, and no case files would be needed. Instead, the regulation provides that recreation is to be provided to "help meet specific individual therapeutic needs in self-expression and social interaction," that is, as part of the professional casework plan.

In addition, there are 11 services that can be analyzed in the same manner as chore services. On the surface, they appear to be self-defined services valuable in their own right (such as recreation) and not requiring justification by a casework plan. Some are mundane, like chore services, and others require sophisticated professionals to perform them. These services include family planning, home and financial management, housing services, information and referral, legal services, personal care services, sheltered employment, and transportation. The regulations are silent as to all of these services; thus, they are in exactly the same position as chore services. Are they to be given merely for the asking, and is this the proper measure of success? Or are they to be given only as part of a casework plan? In fact, there will be great variation, but the decisions will be discretionary, of low visibility and, for the most part, locked in the breasts of the field-level social workers and their supervisors. Silence in the written law has created discretion and delegated it to the social workers. Choices have been made by default, to the detriment of both clients and quality controllers.

Solutions to the Discretion Problem

Although the issues involved in the choices between specific and vague rules have been clarified, the solutions remain elusive. Each service must be evaluated not only in terms of the worth of the service itself (for example, do we want to pay for chore services?) but also in terms of its legal and administrative consequences. As I discussed, there are some services which have to remain vaguely defined, and their delivery will have to be left to the professional discretion of the social workers. Counseling, for example, cannot be specified in a rule, nor should it be. There are other services that will remain vaguely defined because we lack the ability to be specific; either we cannot agree on who should get the service or we cannot forecast the future and are afraid of creating hardships. In such a situation, the prudent course is to proceed on a case-by-case basis, requiring the dispensers of the service to keep careful records, and to refine the rule periodically to chart the boundaries of discretion.

In the allocation of public housing, for example, if a certain number of units are to be designated for families in stress, then careful monitoring is called for to help insure uniform treatment by social workers. Similarly situated families should not be treated differently because they happen to have different social workers. A carefully tailored review-and-appeal system ought to be established to replace the regular welfare department fair hearing system, and there could be a small number of housing units reserved for emergencies for families who do not fit the stated criteria but who obviously need housing to prevent further familial disintegration. Rules of this type should be periodically reconsidered and redrafted with the goal of providing specificity to the greatest possible extent consistent with policy goals.

Finally, there are services where results should be measured by the delivery of the service itself, and the regulation should clearly specify this fact. For the reasons already spelled out, leaving the matter vague or tacking on rehabilitative goals involves serious legal and administrative consequences. Careful records can be kept on the allocation of the services, but their provision should not be dependent on acceptance of a casework plan. If rationing is called for, then, as in the housing example, the criteria should be spelled out as clearly as possible.

Creating specific rules is not an easy task, but it does not have to be done wholesale. What must be done first is to recognize why specificity is important, and what is to be gained or lost by being specific. Then the services should be approached one by one, with full recognition of the fact that for many services it is inappropriate or not feasible to be specific. The second thing to keep in mind is that regulations are not carved in stone; they should be monitored, evaluated, and amended to take account of new information.

One possible solution to low-visibility, open-ended rules is to use the contract system for casework. This system, which was popular in some social work agencies a few years ago, requires the social worker and client to enter into a contract that details the terms of the relationship. For example, if the client attends a certain number of sessions, then the caseworker will do certain things like seeing a school teacher on behalf of one of the children (Maluccio and Marlow, 1974; Stein et al., 1974). In practice, it has been difficult to implement the contract system, but in theory it does hold promise for ameliorating some of the problems discussed. Presumably, if the social worker must specify what he is required to deliver, he might be more cautious in his promises and might concentrate on more simple, mundane tasks that the client and the quality controllers can evaluate. The problem, though, is providing incentives to induce the social worker to make specific promises of simple things that can be measured by both clients and supervisors. One incentive might be that the client would be more willing to participate in the relationship, but since social workers have discretionary authority over goods that clients need and want anyway, they already have the means to induce clients to participate. Other incentives could come from the supervisors. Management could insist that the casework file show evidence that the social worker has agreed to perform certain kinds of tasks in return for client participation. However, management has been unwilling to press for contract-type arrangements. Social work staffs have resisted such precise agreements because, as discussed, they tend to deprofessionalize the social worker as well as to expose him to more accurate monitoring. Perhaps, too, management has doubts as to how much it wants to learn given the high costs, including loss of morale.

THE ORGANIZATION OF SOCIAL SERVICES

In addition to the character of the rules, the organization of the social services delivery system has an important bearing on the problems of discretion, client protection, and quality control. Social services have developed in a variety of settings. Various public agencies offer social services in support of their main duties; there are school, hospital, housing, and prison social workers. Other public agencies offer specialized social services, such as family planning and counseling, child protection, and employment training. There are also publicly provided "hard" services, such as day care, chore services, and meals-on-wheels. In addition, there is the very important private or voluntary sector, which usually concentrates on family counseling, and psychiatric and psychological services. The organizational issue centers on the extent to which this diverse system (or nonsystem) should be coordinated and integrated.

Integration of Services in Great Britain

One justification for the integration of social services is based on the idea of the multiproblem family. In Chapter 1 I described the work of Bradley Buell and his firm, Community Research Associates (CRA), and their use of the term *multiproblem family*. Since the problems (symptoms) of a family are interrelated, there are compelling reasons for the careful integration of social services.

In Great Britain, similar ideas of the interrelatedness of family problems gained currency at roughly the time of the CRA reports. The work of the Pacifist Service Units with bombed-out families during World War II was described in a book by T. Stephens called *Problem Families* (1945). Stephens argued that low standards in the home produce the specific symptoms that bring families to particular social services agencies, but that rather than deal with only one symptom of disintegration (the presenting problem), the agencies should treat all the symptoms equally and treat the underlying causes as well. Instead, said Stephens, social services often entered the picture too late, and because they only treated one specific symptom, they were either ineffectual or worked at cross purposes. He called for more coordination between the services and brought to public attention the idea of "family casework."

Other British reports picked up on Stephens's themes. The Women's Group on Public Welfare, in its report *The Neglected Child and His Family* (1948), addressed the question of what factors in the home led to family breakup and concluded that rarely was the lack of material goods the cause. Rather, the critical problem was the lack of capacity of the mother; it was the combination of "inadequate equipment, mental and material, to deal with problems which would tax even those highly endowed [p. 47]" which led to family disintegration. Throughout the 1950s other studies came to the same conclusion; namely, the family as a whole, rather than specific symptoms, had to be treated, and social services ought to be reorganized so as to be able to better deal with the basic problems of family functioning (Handler, 1973; Philp and Timms, 1962). David Donnison, in his empirical study (1954) of the impact of social services, concluded that the failure of social services was not due primarily to the lack of early detection but rather to the jurisdictional boundaries of the separate services. Quite often, families seeking help had problems beyond the jurisdiction of the particular agency they contacted, and often these other problems constituted a more serious detriment to the family. All observers came to the conclusion that the symptoms commonly used to describe the problem family—marital breakdown, delinquency, neglect, ill health, mental problems—were really symptoms of deeper problems. For social services to be effective, they had to be preventive. Therefore, the separate social services had to be reorganized so that they could treat families as a whole.

At first the British Government moved by stages along the path called for by the scholars and social reform organizations (see Handler, 1973, chaps. 2–4). Then, in 1968, after 3 years of study and deliberation, the influential Seebohm report was issued (Report of the Committee on Local Authority and Allied Personal Social Services, 1968). It called for the creation of a public general family service to provide a unified approach to many of the social services presently offered families. The report was followed by legislation establishing local Social Service Departments, whose functions included traditional child protection (i.e., adoptions, care of orphans, and foster care); preventive child protection services for problem families; programs for the blind, deaf, dumb, and otherwise physically and mentally handicapped persons; residential programs for the aged, infirm, needy, and homeless; health and mental services for expectant, unsupported, and nursing mothers; the provision of home help and day care; and guardianship for the mentally ill. Although the powers of the reorganized Social Services Department were extensive and much more comprehensive than anything then existing either in Great Britain or in the United States, they were still not complete; for example, the administration of juvenile justice and the health services remained separate.[7]

Reorganizing Services in the United States

In the United States, the organization of social services remains fragmented but the trend has followed the British example. It will be recalled

---

[7]For a review of further developments in the British reorganization, see Hall (1976).

that in the early part of the 1960s, the social work profession persuaded Congress that at least part of the welfare dependency problem could be cured by the use of public social services to rehabilitate families; accordingly, social services became part of the AFDC program. The marriage proved unsatisfactory for a variety of reasons; the profession welcomed the public money but quickly saw that the burdens of becoming part of a complex public bureaucracy clearly outweighed the benefits. The profession was also embarrassed when its claims for the rehabilitative powers of social services (principally family casework) were obviously unfulfilled. The profession then called for a separation of social services from public assistance, but with continued public support for social services.

There were two basic approaches in the new thinking about the organization of social services. One was that services had to be universal, meaning that although special provisions should be made for the poor and otherwise disadvantaged, in general social services should be available to the entire population. The profession argued that services restricted to the poor would inevitably become poor services. The second point was that services should be reorganized on an integrated, comprehensive basis.

In 1968, Wilbur Cohen, then Secretary of HEW, convened a task force on the organization of social services. The task force criticized social services for being "problem centered"—that is, for developing programs by identifying a particular problem (e.g., delinquency or mental retardation) and creating a service to deal specifically with that problem. This practice resulted in ad hoc, unplanned development rather than in the careful consideration of priorities; consequently, there was lack of coordination among the various services, people did not know where to go, and there were inefficiencies in the delivery of services. The task force called for a temporary moratorium on expansion or for the creation of single-purpose agencies and asked that priority be given to the development of "a cohesive, coordinative" social service.

Although the task force report was never published, the new Republican administration followed recommendations for the reorganization of social services. In the Nixon administration's proposed Title XX (1970), which was never enacted, the functions of social services were expanded and the foundations were laid for the development of an integrated service. State governments were encouraged to submit plans for the consolidation of health, education, and welfare services and eventually to provide services through single sites.

The present Title XX avoids the issues of centralization versus decentralization by leaving the matter, at present, up to the discretion of the states and HEW. Nevertheless, the call for integration continues. So far, the only practical influence exerted by multiproblem family concepts is the sporadic growth of local, multiservice neighborhood centers. But these centers are laregely concerned with access information, advice, referral, education, advocacy, and follow-up. Their principal failure is that they lack command over an integrated service network; thus, although they can help, they cannot deliver. In the words of Alfred Kahn (1976), "Most of the more ambitious multi-service centers have offered little more than centralized intake, perhaps supplemented by shared records. . . . One major study showed that despite the multiple needs of clients entering multiservice centers, very few received more than one service [p. 23]." (See also Kammerman and Kahn, 1976.) Kahn argues that integration on the field level, through case records or information—advocacy systems, is doomed to failure unless there is also integration of social services programs at the state or federal level.

Like Kahn and other professional-social-work spokesmen, the National Conference on Social Work Task Forces on the Organization and Delivery of Human Services, in its report entitled *Current Issues in Title XX Programs (1976)*, assumes the desirability of a comprehensive, integrated system and addresses itself to the question of how to create such a system. A comprehensive delivery system would be responsible for clarifying the problems of clients, formulating objectives, identifying the services to be provided, and estimating the resources—in short, planning and managing the social services system. The task force called for the state Title XX agencies to assume this management role, to "act as a link between the client and other resources, and to . . . orchestrate a variety of service alternatives in addition to providing certain 'hard' services [p. 11]." The key to this process is the development of what is called the "case-management system." A case manager is a social worker who is trained and financed by the Title XX agency to act as a "manager—broker" for the client. In this role, the case manager will help "move the present system toward the comprehensiveness that would bring both efficiency and effectiveness to service delivery [p. 11]." The case manager is supposed to analyze the "presenting problem in context," to identify, develop, and prescribe the service needed, to coordinate the delivery of the prescribed services, and to "maintain ultimate responsibility for service delivery [p. 12]." The development of this system would place the Title XX agency in a central role. The agency would be accountable for the funds, and its officer, the case manager, would be the person accepting the client, specifying the program, and either administering the program himself if the required services were available from the Title XX agency or arranging for the service from a contracting provider agency. An example given by the task force is that of a person discharged from a mental institution. A case manager would be assigned and would be responsible for services such as housing, food, health, recreation, supervision by the mental health agency, and retraining. The case manager would be not only a referrer–broker, but would also act as a social work supervisor and monitor of the providing agency's performance. Since the case manager works for the Title XX agency, he presumably would carry authority with the provider agency.

The task force made other recommendations designed to strengthen the role of the Title XX agency in its attempts to create a comprehensive system. Although under present legislation the Title XX agencies lack authority over other state statutory service agencies, the task force said that the Title XX agency should in no case be merely a conduit for funds to other service agencies. Rather, the Title XX agency should use its funds either to provide services directly or to contract with provider agencies for services. In this case, the provider agency would be fully accountable to the Title XX agency. Concerning the mix of public and private agencies, the task force recommended that local conditions should determine the pattern of delivery; that is, there should not be a predetermined legislative position as to which type of agency, public or private, should deliver which kind of service in the various jurisdictions. However, even within this framework of pluralism and competition, the Title XX agency would assume a primary supervisory role. The Title XX agency would be charged with the "primary responsibility for guaranteeing the availability—and accounting for the provision—of basic social services," and the all-important functions of case management, case assignment, and evaluation would be the responsibility of the Title XX agency.

As part of its responsibility for the accountability of the provider agencies, the task force said that the Title XX agencies should be responsible for defining the quality of the services provided and for the required documentation. The latter raises the troublesome issues of privacy versus the need for quality control information discussed in Chapter 5. The position taken by the task force was that Title XX agencies have to get information that identifies clients by name and provides evidence that services were in fact received. The task force said that the documentation should be used "only for auditing, eligibility, and service evaluation" and that "confidentiality must be protected" (italics in original), but it did not suggest how this was to be done. It did acknowledge that existing regulations provide inadequate protection and suggested that HEW assume responsibility for reviewing state confidentiality safeguards.

In addition, the task force recommended that Title XX agencies retain legal responsibility for eligibility determination for all Title XX services, although it noted that responsibility could be delegated to a properly accountable provider agency, especially where there are different eligibility requirements for different services. However, the case manager should determine eligibility for all services with similar eligibility requirements.

To sum up the argument, the connection between the theory of casework and the organization of social services delivery is that since presenting problems are only symptoms of more fundamental underlying problems, an effective social service has to be able to treat all of the problems and to reach back into the underlying causes if necessary. Therefore, a service cannot be restricted to a single problem but must be comprehensive, or capable of treating all the problems of a family. Under the existing structure, families with multiple problems have to visit several agencies. As a result, there are gaps in the total service delivered, efforts to aid the family are not coordinated, and the various agencies work at cross-purposes. Thus, to make service delivery efficient, there must be comprehensiveness as well as integration. Since Title XX does not adopt this position, the task force recommended a procedure to help achieve these goals—the case manager system. But the task force made an important addition to the case manager plan by giving the Title XX agencies supervisory and quality control responsibilities; the case managers supplied by Title XX would thus have authority and leverage in their bargaining with the provider agencies.

Before turning to an analysis of the comprehensive, integrated approach, it is necessary to discuss the relationship between the structure of rules and this form of social services delivery system. If the eligibility and performance criteria of specific Title XX services are simplified, the arguments in favor of a comprehensive, integrated service are considerably weakened. An employment service could provide day care positions for the children of people who were placed in jobs; housing agencies could provide home management, budgeting, and chore services. There would still be a need for information, referral, and advocacy, but because each component would allocate its particular service on the basis of simplified eligibility, and because each would be evaluated in terms of the delivery of that service, there would be no need for either comprehensiveness or integration. The idea behind both comprehensiveness and integration is to avoid working at cross-purposes when dealing with multiproblem families. Only insofar as specific services are considered part of a general rehabilitation program is there need for comprehensiveness and integration.

Comprehensiveness and integration, and especially the case manager system, maximize management supervision and the central role of the social work profession. Much of the debate and political fighting over the British reorganization involved these issues. The separate services, particularly those with an established professional base, such as health, education, and mental health, viewed the Seebohm Report as a power play by the Children's Service. The report of the task force on Title XX will be viewed in much the same light. If the state Title XX agencies emerge as an important source of additional funds for various statutory services, such as mental health clinics, day care centers, training centers, and legal services, then proposals to make the Title XX agencies more than mere conduits by giving them accounting responsibilities backed up by the case manager will be viewed quite properly as the assertion of powerful levers over these agencies.

Comprehensiveness and integration have important implications for client protection. I have defined client dependency in terms of discretion, that is, the extent to which a client needs and wants goods that may be granted or not at an official's discretion, with or without conditions. The case manager, as envisaged by the Title XX task force, is a person of enormous discretionary power. He is the principal eligibility officer, he receives the application, he evaluates what is necessary, and he defines the casework plan. Moreover, he manages the casework plan; he either gives direct service or arranges for provider agencies to deliver the services. Finally, he is responsible for evaluating results. If the case manager functions according to the task force plan, the family will be enormously dependent on him, since he is the principal dispenser of all the goods and services that the family needs and wants. The family would not dare to challenge or cross this person. From a legal and administrative point of view, comprehensiveness and integration within the case manager system means a centralization and monopolization of discretionary power in one agency and one official and thus a significant increase in power over clients.

From the client's perspective, it can be argued that the present Title XX system increases client protection because it offers alternatives. Thus, at least in theory, a powerful control that a client has over a social service agency is exit: If the client does not like the conditions put on the service he can leave and go somewhere else. In a competitive situation this can be an important lever. Agencies compete for Title XX dollars and at refunding time they have to show results; thus, they need clients and especially clients who will succeed (however success is defined). If clients are aware of their power and of alternatives, then they are in a position to bargain with the agency. In a comprehensive integrated system, or even with an effective case manager system, this power is reduced substantially.

Structural Models for Change

Verdon Staines (1976) has presented a model for the delivery of social services that attempts to introduce competitive elements throughout the structure. Staines, looking at social services as an industry, argues that great discretion is analogous to the market power of monopolies. The social services "industry" is "characterized by a small number of major suppliers who consciously seek not to compete with one another, severe restrictions on new entry, behavior by each firm which virtually insures the demand for its product, and passivity and ignorance about both the product and the industry among nearly all customers [p. 3]." The opposite situation is competition, where market forces limit the discretion of the various economic units. Staines argues that a competitive strategy can be used as a means of controlling discretion in social services either in lieu of or in conjunction with a legal strategy of fair hearings. His proposal is elaborate and only the basic features will be presented.

Staines separates the social service delivery system into three distinct stages: (a) eligibility determination, (b) providing the means to acquire benefits, and (c) the delivery of benefits. Competition would be introduced at each stage. Eligibility determinations would be made not only by government welfare agencies, but also by privately run "authorized social service agencies." Determinations would be made according to detailed codes; accuracy would be encouraged by financial incentives, including payment for discovering the underauthorization of services. Clients would be free to choose any agency or authorized eligibility specialist. Once eligibility had been determined, vouchers would be issued. The vouchers would be redeemable at public and private agencies that agreed to honor them.

How would competitive constraints on discretion work at each of these stages? At the eligibility stage, the authorized social services agency would be licensed by the government to not only make eligibility determinations but also to provide social services under the government programs. They would be paid according to the number of cases handled and the value of the benefits delivered, but they would be penalized for wrongful eligibility determinations or for the overauthorization of benefits. Penalties would be based on percentages of error. The incentives would be to try to get the maximum eligibility authorized by law.

The authorized eligibility agencies would first make a determination of general eligibility to participate in the social services program. This decision, supported by documentation, would then be forwarded to a government "Eligibility Review Board," which could reject the determination. If rejected, the authorized agency and the client would have a right to an administrative appeal before an independent hearing officer. Staines would also penalize an agency if too many of its eligibility requests were successfully denied by the Eligibility Review Board. The proposed hearing structure would benefit the client more than the present fair hearing system does, because the authorized eligibility agency would have a financial incentive to vindicate its decision; the hearing would then involve a contest between two "socially reputable bureaucracies" rather than between the client and the agency.

After general eligibility to participate had been determined, the client would have to be declared eligible for special social services items. While Staines does not set forth a specific code of conditions, he does make a number of suggestions for determining eligibility for certain kinds of services and for periodic updating. This code would then be applied to each client to determine eligibility for specific services. Again, the agency would be compensated for the value of benefits, but would be penalized for over- or underauthorization of services.

Agency files would be examined by sample audit but also by "social services eligibility specialists," who would search particularly for underauthorizations and who would be compensated according to some fraction of the value of the underauthorization uncovered. If an underauthorization were uncovered, the agency would be given an opportunity to make a correction or to contest the determination. The client would be notified and directed either to the agency willing to make the correction or to another agency, and the eligibility specialist would be responsible for follow-up. As Staines points out, one of the advantages of using eligibility specialists is that the need for them varies inversely with the average accuracy of the eligibility determinations; the more errors, the more the specialists are able to operate profitably.

What about situations where discretion is needed—for unsatisfactory home conditions that have not been accounted for in the eligibility codes, or for rehabilitative services where, for reasons already stated, specification is not fruitful? In the first situation, Staines would allow agencies a certain amount of noncode, discretionary expenditure per quarter, with review by higher-level government committees. Eligibility specialists would be compensated for successfully encouraging clients to seek funds in this way. Rehabilitation grants would also be fixed by certain percentage amounts per quarter, with review, but with the additional requirement that they could only be made after a decision by a trained social worker.

Once eligibility had been determined, the information would be processed and a statement of authorized benefits issued to the client, who would then receive vouchers redeemable at any authorized public or private agency that provided the appropriate goods or services. The voucher system would determine the actual delivery system. For certain items, Staines would encourage savings by allowing a client to keep a certain fraction of any savings. For example, if a voucher was for a $200 refrigerator, and the client was able to purchase a satisfactory one for $100, the client would be entitled to keep, say, $50.

There remains the question of client information, or awareness on the part of recipients of the availability of benefits and alternative agencies. Staines thinks that the financial incentives provided the eligibility specialists would help promote such awareness, but he also suggests supplementary sources of publicity, such as newsletters, notices, and advertisements.

What is especially important is that Staines' model does not rely on conventional types of information to enhance the competitive elements of the system. Conventional models, which rely merely on the dissemination of information, assume that the information will be received and processed by the consumer who will then exercise choice. The assumption is that if clients have the necessary information about the availability and quality of social services, they will shop for the services that best fulfill their needs. In short, there will be a kind of social services market in which clients will pick and choose. These are highly doubtful assumptions. We know very little about how lay people seek out professional services (see Ladinsky, 1976), but the little evidence available does not indicate that a market process operates. People who seek out doctors and lawyers have little objective information as to price and quality; they select professionals on the basis of word of mouth and rarely, if ever, shop around. If the same behavior is true in social services, and there is no reason to think otherwise, then the existence of a competitive delivery system might not make any difference in enhancing client protection. Staines recognizes the problems of merely disseminating information and therefore supplements the information system by giving the eligibility specialists and the social services agencies themselves a profit incentive. It is to their self-interest to bring in clients, since they are compensated on the basis of how much business they do. Are there other structural arrangements that can better protect clients and at the same time achieve efficiency in the delivery system? One suggestion is to vary the structural location of the case manager. The position of the Title XX case manager, as broker–advocate for the client, is that of one institutional advocate confronting institutional agencies on behalf of a one-time client. His situation is analogous to that of a criminal lawyer representing an accused client in his dealings with the prosecutor, or a personal injury lawyer representing an accident victim in his dealings with an insurance company. The lawyer is a repeat player in the sense that even though he represents this particular client only once, he continues to represent other, similarly situated clients before the same institutions. In this situation, as is well known, the lawyer is under pressure to preserve his bargaining leverage for later cases. The insurance company adjuster may ask the lawyer to accept a lower settlement on this case because he is under pressure from his superiors, with the understanding that he will make it up to the lawyer in the next case. The Title XX case manager is in exactly this position; he is more worried about maintaining his long-term credibility and viability with the provider agencies than with fighting hard for a particular client. At the same time, of course, the provider agencies have to maintain good relations with the case manager, especially if he represents the monitoring agency; in that event, the provider agency may be more prone to bend to the wishes of the case manager. However, in his monitoring role as well, the case manager needs information and cooperation from the provider agencies if he is going to be able to perform his job well. With institutional advocates, the incentives run in favor of maintaining the organization's long-term relationships; in a given situation, this may or may not coincide with the best interests of the client. The important point is that the client's interests are not paramount with repeat players.

Would it make any difference for client loyalty and protection if the case manager was not part of the Title XX agency? Case managers could be employed by other public agencies, by private agencies, or by private entrepreneurs. They could be full-time employees, salaried and under contract, or they could be compensated according to the amount of work they did. The argument is that the funding source would affect the worker's loyalties and performance. Thus, private agency workers would worry about the elites that support traditional charity; community-based organizations would be responsive to their boards or to the power behind the board, such as a community group or the local political party. Private entrepreneurs would be paid by the clients; presumably they would be more accountable since their business would depend on their ability to attract and deliver services to clients. But how would the private entrepreneurs be paid? Various proposals have been made for social insurance for the poor or for vouchers.[8]

Varying the structural location of the case manager involves some important assumptions and trade-offs. One assumption concerns the impact of competition discussed earlier. Accountability to clients depends on the agency's need to recruit clients and deliver services. Although this is clearly the basis for the private entrepreneur argument, it also underlies the rationale for using other agencies since they too have to get business; the theory is that they can only attract clients if they deliver. As indicated earlier, the market analogy might not be accurate; there are information problems and lack of knowledge as to how clients select professional services. The guess is that, generally, competition among social service agencies would work to the advantage of the client, but no one is really sure of this.

But a more serious objection is that even with a different structural location, the case manager is still an institutional advocate. Whether he is an employee of a public or private agency, or a private entrepreneur, he still must deal repeatedly with the same agencies on behalf of different clients. Moreover, the case manager would lack the institutional clout derived from his employment by the Title XX agency. If the Title XX agency is concerned with establishing its power and control over provider agencies and with ferreting out their weaknesses, then presumably the case manager would act aggressively on behalf of the clients. This would be analogous to the Wisconsin district directors' performance discussed in Chapter 3. On the other hand, the Title XX agency may be politically weak and may need the support and goodwill of the provider agencies; in this event, the case manager would be more interested in maintaining these relations than in aggressive representation.

Another possible structural variation has been proposed by Margaret Rosenheim (1976). Rosenheim uses juvenile "nuisances" as her example, but she offers her proposal as being generally applicable to social services as well. Rosenheim claims that one of the major difficulties with social services is their tendency to "problemize" what are ordinary, conventional

---

[8]Alternative structural arrangements, including private entrepreneurs, are discussed in Piliavin (1971). See also Piliavin et al. (1972).

personal troubles. The traditional welfare model, as discussed in Chapter 1, views the individual or family in pathological terms and employs individual treatment to restore healthy functioning. Problemization, in Rosenheim's terms, is related to the welfare model but focuses on the agency—the organization and the professionals who formulate the view of the client and then act upon that view. According to Rosenheim, problemization is a basic characteristic of specialists; "having command of the knowledge thought useful to solve a group of problems is likely to be a potent influence on the expert's perception of the conditions or problems presented by seekers of help [p. 179]." Moreover, not only is problemization a natural outgrowth of specialization, but experts find extreme cases most interesting and challenging, and this is where the contribution of the expert is most clearly valued. As a consequence, theories supporting intervention tend to give disproportionate weight to the most unique or bizarre troubles falling within the ambit of the particular specialist. In Rosenheim's words, "The boundaries of specialization not only frame the diagnostic process but also frame the structure of service [pp. 179–180]."

Rosenheim argues that the treatment of juvenile nuisances is a prime example of how problemization has worked badly. Juvenile nuisances are defined by exclusion; they are minors who are neither seriously criminal nor severely disturbed. The category includes petty thieves, runaways, truants, bullies, and the like. Although the numbers vary, they are usually the majority of all children dealt with by the juvenile court. Disenchantment with the juvenile court approach to nuisances is based on growing evidence that this form of delinquency is "normal" and temporary, that labeling may have a deleterious influence, and that rehabilitation can result in coercive interventions which often serve organizational needs rather than the needs of the child. Yet neither courts nor juvenile services treat this kind of low-level delinquency as normal. They either shunt aside these cases or treat them as problems. This attitude has particularly harsh consequences for the poor. All people have personal troubles, but whereas the better off have the means to sort out their troubles privately, the poor become involved in some kind of "problem formulation" process. If they need more help, then they become known as a multiproblem family, which, Rosenheim argues, is an artifact of the organization of services. The various problems are labeled for treatment by law, medicine, training, or some other method. We insist on isolating and categorizing personal troubles as problems even though many of these troubles, like those of juvenile nuisances, would yield to palliatives (a term Rosenheim prefers to *solutions*).

To handle juvenile nuisances, Rosenheim argues for a "normalizing" approach, which looks at nuisance behavior as minor and "rarely persistent or deeply alarming." The task of public policy, then, is not to develop "diagnostic and remedial strategies for exotic cases" but instead to ease the situation. If the behavior is not viewed as especially serious, then "symptomatic response, palliation, and crisis support" are called for instead of diagnosis and prescription. By reducing diagnosis and classification, we also "counterbalance the tendency of officials and professionals to problemize," thus in turn opening up the utilization of nonexperts to help with these nonserious, transient problems. There is no need or "license" to explore other, underlying problems.

Rosenheim sketches a model service organization for the "normal" treatment of juvenile nuisances. She envisages a modest front-line agency which can give help quickly and flexibly, and where "above all, the attitude . . . should be humane, taking each day's events seriously as personal troubles, but not as 'problems' [p. 188]." The overriding service principle, of course, is to view troubles as normal and to recognize that ordinary people have troubles which are not "problems." What, then, do people with normal troubles expect and require? The first thing they expect is for something to be done, a first-aid response, rather than careful, formal diagnosis. However, the response not only should be speedy but also should be helpful. There should also be an initial tendency to accept the client's definition of the trouble. This is part of the normalization approach; if troubles are considered normal, then ordinary people can usually identify them. The Rosenheim model is a modest, first-aid helping service, which should be in close proximity to the people. The social service ought to serve a relatively small geographical area; specialization for more severe troubles can be located farther away and can serve larger geographic areas. Finally, Rosenheim suggests more imaginative use of training, of the telephone, and of transportation for these social first-aid outposts. Panels of experts (lawyers, housing specialists, psychiatrists, etc.) could be linked to the outpost through telephone consultation. When immediate referrals to specialists are needed, circulating minibuses could be used.

How would Rosenheim's proposal apply to the organization of Title XX services, and what effects would it have on the issues of discretion, client protection, and quality control? The staff of this front-line agency would be nonprofessional or less professional than the case manager called for by the Title XX task force. The effort would be to normalize the personal troubles of social service clients. Eligibility rules for the allocation of services would be simple and clear-cut; output would be measured by the service that is delivered, not by the success of a rehabilitation plan. What resources would such an agency have at its disposal? It would have all of the information-access resources—brokering, referral, advocacy, and the telephone and transportation links that Rosenheim suggests. It could also have a supply of hard services—chore services, home helps, day care facilities, and temporary shelter for families, adults, or children. The agency could also have emergency cash assistance. Long-term day care and shelter would probably be handled by other agencies; this agency would be a first-aid facility designed to get people over temporary hurdles.

The staff of the agency would differ from the Title XX task force case manager only to the extent that the professional and organizational incentives differed. To what extent would Rosenheim's staff tend to normalize or problemize, and how would their approach differ from that of the case manager? Arguments in favor of a normalization approach would emphasize that the agency ultimately would depend on recruitment from the community and so would have to deliver services and establish a reputation in the community for sympathy and quick response. Dependent upon the community, the agency would tend to accept the client's definition of the problem and dispense hard services with a minimum of intrusive intervention. Because the agency would be only one among several social service agencies in the community, it would be in a competitive situation, unlike the case manager, who is in a monopoly situation. According to the Title XX task force, the case manager is the principal gate-keeper for all Title XX services in the jurisdiction, even though the actual services may be delivered under contract with a provider agency. Therefore, the case manager does not have to seek out business; he either gets the walk-in trade or it is referred to him by clients who first knock on the door of other social service agencies that receive Title XX funds. This would not be the case with Rosenheim's first-aid agencies.

Because of their competitive posture, the first-aid agencies would tend to normalize troubles in order to keep business; problemization would mean a referral. The first-aid staff's incentives would be to handle as many problems as they could as a matter of organizational pride and profit; this would mean resolving requests simply and reporting successful closings. On the other hand, they would also have to form relationships with specialist agencies because some clients would have more serious problems or would require resources not at the disposal of the first-aid agency. Therefore, the first-aid staff would inevitably become institutional advocates as well as client advocates. However, because they lack the monopoly position of the case manager and are more dependent on client goodwill, they may be more aggressive in pursuing client interests.

The first-aid staff would have some discretion but considerably less than that of the case manager or professional social worker, principally because eligibility would not be defined in terms of rehabilitative goals. The staff would not feel that giving a client goods and services merely for the asking is nonprofessional. Simple rules and clear-cut criteria would also help to confine discretion. In other words, the incentives of this kind of organization would tend to reduce discretion rather than increase it as in a professionally staffed agency or in the case manager model. The ability of a client to challenge the exercise of that discretion should also be greater in the first-aid agency. Clearly stated rules would give the client an advantage, but more importantly, the client would have the power of exit; he could take his business elsewhere if he did not like the terms and conditions of the service. Because the first-aid staff person would not occupy a monopoly position, the client would run less risk if he challenged the agency's decision.

Monitoring and evaluation problems also seem somewhat easier under Rosenheim's model. As stated, her model presents a conflict or competitive situation between the nonprofessional first-aid agency and the professional specialist agency. The tendency of the first-aid agency to normalize troubles as a way of increasing the value of their organization plays into the hands of the evaluators, since the emphasis is on simplified eligibility and measurable output. There would be a disclosure of information about what the staff considers to be normal troubles with normal palliatives. As pointed out, the incentives for the professional social worker are the opposite; because they adopt a rehabilitative approach and have difficulty in delivering or proving the value of their service, they are better off withholding information or masking it in discretionary, low-visibility decisions.

With the Title XX task force case manager, it is difficult to predict which way the evaluation incentives run. He is in a powerful position to evaluate the provider agencies but he may also need their services. On the other hand, he is an employee of the principal evaluating agency, the Title XX agency, and this presents obvious conflicts. With Rosenheim's model, there are now conflicts and competition among three agency structures— the first-aid agency, the specialist agencies, and the Title XX agency. Both the Title XX agency and the specialist agencies have incentives to carefully evaluate the first-aid agency. There is the fight over obtaining business, and there are also professional conflicts; the first-aid agency would tend to normalize troubles, whereas the professionals in the Title XX agency and the specialist agencies tend to problemize. It is my guess that both the quality controllers and the clients would benefit from these conflicts. The situation is analogous to the Wisconsin State District Director System described in Chapter 3. There, the district directors used clients' fair hearing complaints not only to protect the clients but as a means of discovering weaknesses in county administration. Hopefully, a similar situation would prevail here as each agency attempted to justify its activities and cast aspersions on the activities of the others.

At this stage in our knowledge, the effects of all of these structural alternatives are speculative. An imaginative investigator could probably find existing or historical models for the various alternatives scattered throughout the country, but there has been little, if any, research done to evaluate what impact these structures have on staff and client behavior. What I have tried to point out is that despite the importance of structure for the exercise of discretion, for the protection of clients, and for the control of field-level activity, these considerations are rarely raised in discussions of the organization of social services.

SUMMARY

In Part II, a number of possibilities for improving client protection have been canvassed. Some alternatives look to strengthening the resources of the client; these include professional and lay advocacy services that assume the continued existence of the adversary system for client protection. Other approaches look to remedies that do not rely on the adversary model and may hold promise for social services clients. These include various forms of ombudsmen and mediation–arbitration procedures. The essential idea is that an independent official is charged with investigating complaints or other kinds of administrative problems and with negotiating a settlement. For the dependent client, the ombudsman system offers many advantages, the principal one being that it is the ombudsman who assumes the burden of working up the factual investigation and presenting the case. A number of investigative arbitration programs already exist in a variety of settings, and they should be examined in terms of effectiveness and applicability to social services clients.

Three strategies for strengthening client protection by improving the social services system itself were also explored. Although management and quality control systems are not directly concerned with individual cases, the need for client grievance mechanisms will be lessened to the extent that such systems can reduce administrative error and enforce rules and standards. However, given the present state of development, it seems that there are great difficulties in implementing effective monitoring systems for social services and that current attempts to gather information under present programs pose grave threats to the privacy interests of clients.

The two other strategies deal with rules and with structures, both of which are sources of much unnecessary administrative discretion and arbitrary power over the lives of clients. The problems caused by loose, vague terminology in rules cannot be overemphasized; tacking on catch-all rehabilitative goals for every kind of ordinary service enormously complicates the problems of administrative justice at all levels. Vague standards lessen the ability of a client to present reasoned, relevant evidence in support of his claim and of the reviewing officer or court to effectively change the field-level decision. There is a great need to examine the variety of services offered under Title XX and to decide what conditions should attach to each service. One of the problems, of course, is that social service agencies want to retain the power to grant an otherwise routine or mundane service to a client who does not fit precisely within the eligibility criteria but who nevertheless needs the service for rehabilitative purposes. Here, one of Staines's suggestions might prove useful. He proposes that the agency have a certain proportion of its funds available for extraordinary circumstances and for rehabilitative goals. This would not only provide a more carefully controlled ceiling on the amount of money that could be spent for these purposes, but—and this is the important point—it removes the necessity of adding on rehabilitative or emergency provisions for all of the other services.

Proposals to vary delivery structures are also controversial. Social services planners and administrators have always been appalled at the diversity, complexity, and overlap of programs and have argued that this causes clients undue hardship. On the other hand, centralizing social services can also impose burdens on clients. The monopoly elements in the delivery system increase discretion and lead to, in Rosenheim's terms, problemization. Staines would introduce more competitive elements to reduce discretion, and Rosenheim would deprofessionalize the front-line agencies in an effort to normalize client problems.

Problems of controlling discretion and protecting dependent clients are not readily amenable to simple solutions. Little information is available about the motivations of field-level officials or about the feelings and perceptions of clients. The area is varied, and a high degree of discretion will always be useful and necessary if programs are to function compassionately and intelligently (see Jowell, 1975, pp. 145–146). Therefore, the challenge is to avoid simplistic approaches and to try to experiment with flexible alternatives that seek to adjust conflicting interests and needs. Opportunities to make sensible and meaningful reforms lie on both sides. Social work and other government professionals should more fully appreciate the consequences of delegating discretion for dependent people; at the same time, client advocates can no longer afford to rely on rigid, legalistic adversary models of conflict resolution that fail to serve the interest of the clients or the agencies. A number of alternative forms of client protection procedures are in the planning or implementation stages. These proposals should be evaluated to determine the extent to which they could prove useful to clients of social services programs.

References

Baum, D. 1974. *The welfare family and mass administrative justice.* New York: Praeger.

Blau, P. 1963. *The dynamics of bureaucracy.* Chicago: University of Chicago Press.

Boyer, B. B. 1972. Alternatives to trial-type hearings for resolving complex scientific, economic, and social issues. *Michigan Law Review, 71,* 111.

Bractel, S. 1974. *Judicare, public funds, private lawyers, and poor people.* Chicago: American Bar Foundation.

Brickman, L. 1971. Expansion of the lawyering process through a new delivery system: The emergence and state of legal paraprofessionalism. *Columbia Law Review, 71,* 1153.

Buell, B., and Associates. 1952. *Community planning for human services.* New York: Columbia University Press.

Buell, B., and Associates. 1953. *The prevention of dependency in Winona County, Minnesota.* New York: Community Research Associates.

Buell, B., and Associates. 1954a. *The prevention and control of disordered behavior in San Mateo County, California.* New York: Community Research Associates.

Buell, B., and Associates. 1954b. *The prevention and control of indigent disability in Washington County, Maryland.* New York: Community Research Associates.

Burgess, P. M., Hofstetter, C. R., and Higgs, L. D. 1973. Puerto Rico's citizen feedback program. In A. J. Wyner (Ed.), *Executive ombudsmen in the United States.* Berkeley, Cal.: Institute of Governmental Studies. Pp. 279–304.

Burns, E. 1965. Where welfare falls short. *The Public Interest, 1,* 82–95.

Campbell, D. T. 1977. Reforms as experiments. In F. G. Caro (Ed.), *Readings in evaluation research.* New York: Russell Sage Foundation. Pp. 233–261.

Cappelletti, M. 1975. Governmental and public advocates for public interest in civil litigation. *Michigan Law Review, 73,* 793.

Capps, D. L. 1973. Executive ombudsmen: The Oregon experience. In A. J. Wyner (Ed.), *Executive ombudsmen in the United States.* Berkeley, Cal.: Institute of Governmental Studies. Pp. 189–231.

Chase, C. I., and Pugh, R. C. 1971. Social class and performance on an intelligence test. *Journal of Educational Measurement, 8,* 197–202.

Chitwood, S. R. 1975. Social equity and social service productivity. *Public Administration Review, 35,* 387–395.

Cloward, R. A., and Piven, F. F. 1972. *The politics of turmoil.* New York: Vintage.

Comments. 1976. The freedom of information act's privacy exemption and the privacy act of 1974. *Harvard Civil Rights–Civil Liberties Law Review, 11,* 596.

Congressional Research Service. 1977. *Administration of the AFDC program, A report to the Committee on Government Operations.* Washington, D.C.: U.S. Government Printing Office.

Davis, K. C. 1969. *Discretionary justice: A preliminary inquiry.* Baton Rouge: Louisiana State University Press.

Derthick, M. 1976. Guidelines for social services grants. *Policy Sciences, 7,* 489–504.

DeWoolfson, B. H., Jr. 1975. Public sector MBO and PPB: Cross fertilization in management systems. *Public Administration Review, 35,* 387–395.

Dixon, R. G., Jr. 1973. *Social Security disability and mass justice: A problem in welfare adjudication.* New York: Praeger.

Donnison, D. V. 1954. *The neglected child and the social services.* Manchester: Manchester University Press.

Federal Register, Vol. 41, No. 231. November 30, 1976, p. 52495.

Frank, J. L. 1976. Legal services for citizens of moderate income. In M. L. Schwartz (Ed.), *Law and the American future.* Englewood Cliffs, N.J.: Prentice-Hall. Pp. 116–130.

Frederikson, H. G. 1974. Social equity and public administration. *Public Administration Review, 34,* 1–2.

Friedman, L. 1969. Social welfare legislation: An introduction. *Stanford Law Review, 21,* 217.

Friendly, H. J. 1975. Some kind of hearing. *University of Pennsylvania Law Review, 123,* 1267.

Galanter, M. 1974. Why the haves come out ahead: Speculations on the limits of legal change. *Law and Society Review, 9,* 95.

Gellhorn, W. 1966. *Ombudsman and others.* Cambridge, Mass.: Harvard University Press.

Gellhorn, W. 1967. Poverty and legality: The law's slow awakening. *William and Mary Law Review, 9,* 300.

Gitterman, A., and Germain, C. 1976. Social work practice: A life model. *Social Service Review, 50,* 601.

Hall, P. 1976. *Reforming welfare: The politics of change in the personal social services.* London: Heinemann Educational Books, Ltd.

Hall, R. V. 1972. *Organizations, structure and process.* Englewood Cliffs, N. J.: Prentice-Hall.

Hamilton, G. 1962. Editorial. *Social Work, 7,* 2.

Hammer, R. P., and Hartley, J. M. 1978. Procedural due process and the welfare recipient: A statistical study of AFDC hearings in Wisconsin. *Wisconsin Law Review,* forthcoming.

Handler, J. F., ed. 1964. *Family law and the poor: Essays by Jacobus tenBroek.* Westport, Conn.: Greenwood.

Handler, J. F. 1966. Controlling official behavior in welfare administration. *California Law Review, 54,* 479.

Handler, J. F. 1969. Justice for the welfare recipient: Fair hearings in AFDC, the Wisconsin experience. *Social Service Review, 43,* 12.

Handler, J. F. 1972. *Reforming the poor.* New York: Basic Books.

Handler, J. F. 1973. *The coercive social worker.* Chicago: Rand McNally.

Handler, J. F., and Goodstein, A. 1968. The legislative development of public assistance. *Wisconsin Law Review, 68,* 414.

Handler, J. F., and Hollingsworth, E. J. 1971. *The deserving poor: A study of welfare administration.* Chicago: Markham.

Handler, J. F., Hollingsworth, E. J., and Erlanger, H. 1978. *Lawyers and the pursuit of legal rights.* New York: Academic.

Handler, J. F., and Rosenheim, M. K. 1966. Privacy in welfare: Public assistance and juvenile justice. *Law and Contemporary Problems, 31,* 377–412.

Hannon, P. J. 1973. The Nassau County ombudsman. In A. J. Wyner (Ed.), *Executive ombudsmen in the United States.* Berkeley, Cal.: Institute of Governmental Studies. Pp. 111–133.

Hanus, J., and Relyea, H. 1976. A policy assessment of the privacy act of 1974. *American University Law Review, 25,* 555–586.

Havens, H. S. 1976. MBO and program evaluation, or whatever happened to PPBS? *Public Administration Review, 36,* 40–45.

Heber, R. 1961. Modifications in the manual on terminology and classification in mental retardation. *American Journal of Mental Deficiency, 65,* 499.

Hill, M., and Laing, P. 1978. *Money payments, social work, and supplementary benefits: A study of section one of the 1963 children and young persons act.* University of Bristol, School for Advanced Urban Studies, Paper Number 1.

Hollis, F. 1964. *Casework: A psychosocial therapy.* New York: Random House.

Horst, P., Nay, J. N., Scanlon, J. W., and Wholey, J. S. 1974. Program management and the federal evaluator. *Public Administration Review, 34,* 300–308.

Jaffe, S. 1978. *Conflict resolution and regulation, another look?* New York: Ford Foundation.

Jowell, J. L. 1975. *Law and bureaucracy: Administrative discretion and the limits of legal action.* Port Washington, N.Y.: Dunellen.

Jun, Jong S. 1976. Introduction to a symposium, management by objectives in the public sector. *Public Administration Review, 36,* 1–5.

Kahn, A. J. 1976. Service delivery at the neighborhood level: Experience, theory, and fads. *Social Service Review, 50,* 23.

Kammerman, S. B., and Kahn, A. J. 1976. *Social services in the United States: Policies and programs.* Philadelphia: Temple University Press.

Kirk, S. A. 1962. *Educating exceptional children.* Boston: Houghton Mifflin.

Kirp, D., Buss, W., and Kuriloff, P. 1974. Legal reforms of special education: Empirical studies and procedural proposals. *California Law Review, 62,* 40.

Klaus, W. R. 1976. Civil legal services for the poor. In M. L. Schwartz (Ed.), *Law and the American future.* Englewood Cliffs, N.J.: Prentice-Hall. Pp. 131–142.

Klein, P. 1968. *From philanthropy to social welfare.* New York: Jossey-Bass.

Levine, R. A. 1970. *The poor ye need not have with you: Lessons from the war on poverty.* Cambridge: M.I.T. Press.

Liston, A. M. 1973. The office of Iowa citizen's aide. In A. J. Wyner (Ed.), *Executive om-*

budsmen in the United States. Berkeley, Cal.: Institute of Governmental Studies. Pp.
151–188.

Lubove, R. 1965. *The professional altruist.* Cambridge, Mass.: Harvard University Press.

Lukoff, I. F., and Mencher, S. 1962. A critique of the conceptual foundation of Community
Research Associates. *Social Science Review, 36,* 433.

Macaulay, S. 1966. *Law and the balance of power.* New York: Russell Sage Foundation.

Malluccio, A. N., and Marlow, W. D. 1974. The case for contract. *Social Work, 19,* 28.

Mann, D. E. 1973. Governor's branch offices in Pennsylvania. In A. J. Wyner (Ed.), *Executive ombudsmen in the United States.* Berkeley, Cal.: Institute of Governmental
Studies. Pp. 233–278.

Mashaw, J. L. 1971. Welfare reform and local administration of Aid to Families with Dependent Children in Virginia. *Virginia Law Review, 57,* 818.

Mashaw, J. L. 1974. The management side of due process: Some theoretical and litigation
notes on the assurance of accuracy, fairness, and timeliness in the adjudication of social
welfare claims. *Cornell Law Review, 59,* 772.

Mashaw, J. L. 1976. The Supreme Court's due process calculus for administrative adjudication in *Mathews* v. *Eldridge:* Three factors in search of a theory of value. *University of
Chicago Law Review, 44,* 28.

Mechanic, D. 1962. Sources of power of lower participants in complex organizations. *Administrative Science Quarterly, 7,* 349.

Mills, A. 1949. *An introduction to public welfare.* Boston: D.C. Heath.

Moore, J. E. 1973. Honolulu's Office of Information and Complaint. In A. J. Wyner (Ed.),
Executive ombudsmen in the United States. Berkeley, Cal.: Institute of Governmental
Studies. Pp. 45–69.

Morris, R. 1964. Editorial. *Social Work, 9,* 2.

National Conference on Social Work Task Forces on the Organization and Delivery of
Human Services. 1976. *Current issues in Title XX programs.* Washington, D. C.

Newman, E., and Turem, J. 1974. The crisis of accountability. *Social Work, 19,* 5–16.

New York State Commission. 1972. *Report on the quality, cost, and financing of elementary
and secondary education.*

Nordlinger, E. A. 1973. Boston's little city halls: Citizens as clients. In A. J. Wyner (Ed.),
Executive ombudsmen in the United States. Berkeley, Cal.: Institute of Governmental
Studies. Pp. 71–110.

O'Neil, R. 1970. *The price of dependency.* New York: E. P. Dutton.

Philp, A. F., and Timms, N. 1962. *The problem of "the problem family."* London: The
Family Service Units.

Piliavin, I. 1971. Provision of social service to recipients of income maintenance. In L. Orr,
R. Hollister, and J. Lefcowitz (Eds.), *Income maintenance.* Chicago: Markham.

Piliavin, I., Handler, J. F., and Hollingsworth, E. J. 1972. Alternatives for delivery of social
services: A research design and experiment. Final report of the social services delivery
project, working project D-2. University of Chicago School of Social Service Administration.

Poland, O. F. 1974. Program evaluation and administrative theory. *Public Administration
Review, 34,* 333–338.

Prottas, J. 1978. The power of the street-level bureaucrat in public service bureaucracies.
Urban Affairs Quarterly, 13, 285–312.

Rabin, R. L. 1970. Implementation of the cost of living adjustment for AFDC recipients: A
case study in welfare administration. *University of Pennsylvania Law Review, 118,* 193.

Rabin, R. L. 1976. Job security and due process: Monitoring administrative discretion through a reasons requirement. *University of Chicago Law Review, 44,* 60.

Reich, C. 1963. Midnight welfare searches and the Social Security Act. *Yale Law Journal, 72,* 1347.

Reich, C. 1964. The new property. *Yale Law Journal, 73,* 733.

Reich, C. 1965. Individual rights and social welfare: The emerging legal issues. *Yale Law Journal, 74,* 1245.

Rein, Mildred. 1975. Social services as work strategy. *Social Service Review, 49,* 515.

Rein, M. 1970. *Social policy: Issues of choice and change.* New York: Random House.

Report of the Committee on Local Authority and Allied Personal Social Services. 1968. H. M. S. O., Cmmd 3703, July.

Report of the Wisconsin Nursing Home Ombudsman Program. 1976. Madison, Wisconsin.

Rivlin, A. M. 1971. *Systematic thinking for social action.* Washington, D.C.: Brookings Institution.

Rosenheim, M. K. 1976. Notes on helping: Normalizing juvenile nuisances. *Social Service Review, 50,* 179–180.

Sapolsky, H. M. 1972. *The polaris system development: Bureaucratic and programmatic success in government.* Cambridge: Harvard University Press.

Sarason, S. 1959. *Psychological problems in mental deficiency.* New York: Harper.

Schick, A. 1973. A death in the bureaucracy: The demise of federal PPB. *Public Administration Review, 33,* 146–156.

Schwartz, B. 1976. Administrative law. Boston: Little, Brown and Co.

Self, P. 1975. *Econocrats and the policy process: The politics and philosophy of cost-benefit analysis.* London: The Macmillan Press.

Sharkansky, I. 1970. *The routines of politics.* New York: Van Nostrand.

Shurn, P., and Parker, J. 1976. An introduction to the federal privacy act of 1974 and its effect on the freedom of information act. *New England Law Review, 11,* 463.

Simon, H. A. 1973. Applying information technology to organization design. *Public Administration Review, 33,* 268–278.

Sinfield, A. 1970. Which way for social work. In *The fifth social service: A critical analysis of the Seebohm proposals.* London: The Fabian Society.

Staines, V. 1976. Administrative discretion in the provision of social services: Its nature, extent, origins, and control. Unpublished manuscript, University of Wisconsin, Madison.

State of Wisconsin. 1977. Wisconsin Department of Health and Social Services, Division of Family Services, County Administration Manual. Madison, Wis.

Stein, T. J., Gambrill, E. D., and Wiltse, R. 1974. Foster care: The use of contracts. *Public Welfare, 32,* 20.

Steiner, G. 1966. *Social insecurity,* New York: Rand McNally.

Stephens, T., ed. 1945. *Problem families: An experiment in social rehabilitation.* London: Pacifist Service Units.

Supplementary Benefits Commission. 1976. Annual Report. HMSO.

tenBroek, J., and Tussman, J. 1949. The equal protection of the laws. *California Law Review, 37,* 341.

Tibbles, L. 1972. Ombudsmen for American prisons. *North Dakota Law Review, 78,* 383.

Trubek, D. 1976. Report on the New Jersey public advocate. Madison, Wis.: Center for Public Representation.

U.S. Department of Health, Education, and Welfare. 1973. *Records, computers, and the rights of citizens,* Report of the Secretary's Advisory Committee on Automated Personal Data Systems. Washington, D.C.: U.S. Government Printing Office.

Van Alstyne, W. W. 1968. The demise of the right–privilege distinction in continental law. *Harvard Law Review, 81,* 1439.

Waldo, D. 1972. Development in public administration. *The Annals of the American Academy of Political and Social Science, 404,* 217–245.

The Washington Post. March 4, 1977, p. D-11.

Weintraub, F. J., and Abeson, A. R. 1972. Appropriate education for all handicapped children: A growing issue. *Syracuse Law Review, 23,* 1037.

Weisbrod, B. A., Handler, J. F., and Komesar, N. (Eds.) 1978. *Public interest law.* Berkeley, Cal.: University of California Press.

Whitford, W. C., and Kimball, S. L. 1974. Why process consumer complaints? A case study of the Office of the Commissioner of Insurance of Wisconsin. *Wisconsin Law Review, 74,* 639.

Wholey, J. S., Scanlon, J. W., Duffy, H. G., Furomoto, J. S., and Vogt, L. M. 1970. *Federal evaluation policy.* Washington, D. C.: Brookings Institution.

Wildavsky, A. 1974. *The politics of the budgetary process.* Boston: Little, Brown. 2nd ed.

Williams, W. 1971. *Social policy research and analysis.* New York: Elsevier Press.

Wilson, J. Q. 1973. *Political organizations.* New York: Basic Books.

Women's Group on Public Welfare. 1948. *The neglected child and his family.* London: National Council of Social Services.

Wyner, A. J. 1973a. Complaining to city hall: The Chicago approach. In A. J. Wyner (Ed.), *Executive ombudsmen in the United States.* Berkeley, Cal.: Institute of Governmental Studies. Pp. 17–44.

Wyner, A. J. 1973b. Lieutenant governors as political ombudsmen. In A. J. Wyner (Ed.), *Executive ombudsmen in the United States.* Berkeley, Cal.: Institute of Governmental Studies. Pp. 135–149.

Yale Law Journal. 1975. Note, The Wyatt case: Implementation of a judicial decree ordering institutional change, *84,* 1338.

Zander, T. K. 1976. Civil commitment procedure in Wisconsin. *Wisconsin Law Review, 76,* 503.